Service comes in many forms. For us it's making self-service easy and pleasurable. For others it is all about personal attention. No matter what style of service is required of your business, this book will help you give your customers what they want.

Geoff Sadler,
Managing Director, K-Mart

We've always held the values in this book as fundamental to our business. Send me forty straight away. You've captured the heart and soul of customer relations and sound business sense.

Denis McFadden,
Managing Director, Just Cuts

The people who work in our stores say the Retail Success Series books are easy to read because they relate to real life and everyday experiences. Yet again, Five Star Service... is a thought provoking book full of the basics – and very informative.

John Charlton,
Managing Director, Spend-Less Shoes

From now on when people ask me for the secret of our eighty five years in business – and our continued growth I'll just hand them this book and say, 'It's all in here'.

Warren Schirmer,
General Manager, Open Book

There are two things that can make one of our franchisees stand out from the crowd. The first is making and selling great muffins and good coffee. The other is the magic quality that draws people up to the counter and promises them joy, relief from stress and a haven from a busy day. You call it 'other' in your book. You're right. It is the essential ingredient.

Bob Nelson,
Managing Director Muffin Break.

As usual you make learning fun and informative. Congratulations on capturing the spirit of customer service in this easily digestible format. The stories and the exercises make it easy to get the message – Give the customers what they want.

Garry Donoghue,
Managing Director, Paper Plus NZ

Whether selling suits as I did for 20 years or managing a thriving community church of eighteen hundred people, the passionate attitudes of the Five Star people you describe in this book are essential. I have personally told your story of the Five Star Man all over the world.

Danny Gugglielmucci,
President, Assemblies of God (SA)

This book hits the spot! It's fun – and the service element is just what retailers need. Following this advice they can't go wrong.

John Maddison,
National Retail Manager, Cue

RETAIL SUCCESS SERIES

★ ★ ★ ★ ★

Five Star Service On a One Star Budget

DEDICATION

For my brothers,

Fred and Jim,

whom I love dearly

and who find it so hard to believe that people actually pay

to hear their little brother talk.

RETAIL SUCCESS SERIES

★ ★ ★ ★ ★

Five Star Service On a One Star Budget

BY COLIN PEARCE

A WESTFIELD RETAIL EDUCATION BOOK

Westfield

WORLD SALES CENTER
ADELAIDE

First published in 1998
World Sales Center
PO Box 303
Unley South Australia 5061

National Library of Australia
Cataloguing-in-Publication entry:

Pearce, Colin (Colin John).
Five star service on a one star budget.

ISBN 0 646 36290 9.

1. Customer services. 2. Customer relations. I. Title.
(Series : Retail success series).

658.812

Cover design and book design: Graeme Cogdell, Imagart Pty Ltd
Cartoons: Paul Duff

Published by World Sales Center, Adelaide
Printed by Openbook Publishers
205 Halifax Street Adelaide SA 5000
1136-98

Contents

THANKYOU

I really value Westfield's participation in this, the second book in the Retail Success Series.

Christine Pressler, my account manager at Open Book where the book was printed is more like a project manager. Thank you.

Graeme Cogdell, is a wonderful art director and Paul Duff makes every story come to life with his zany illustrations. Thanks lads.

Tim Pearce was good on editorial advice. So was my wife, The Lovely Christine, and Irma Schirmer, eagle eyed as ever wins every argument about grammar and punctuation but Oh! so gently.

Thank you also to my friends and clients who have read and endorsed both books and for letting us feature your names and the businesses you represent on the covers.

My biggest thanks go to the thousands and thousands of retailers and their sales teams who took my first book, *Make More Money from Every Sale* so much to heart and who actually put it into practice. I hope this book helps you as much.

FOREWORD

In the highly competitive retail arena, how often do we hear the longing expressed, to be able to afford delivering distinctive customer service?

Fortunately, customer service is not what will cost us and the customer more, but what will provide the customer the most value – and us the healthiest revenues. And when our service delivery is integrated into our business strategies and processes, it is also the most profitable way we can do business.

From his combined experience and deft analysis of the practices of service leaders, Colin Pearce opens our eyes to the realities of service delivery, and thus to the potential, and in fact, the imperative for us to develop our own distinctive, effective and affordable service strategies.

As a long-time retailer and a lifetime student of service delivery, I am grateful to Colin for this most timely and helpful book. I have personally experienced working with retailers as diverse as the globally inspiring fashion retailer, Nordstrom, and the world's largest discounter, Wal-Mart.

Each one of these awesome companies runs on an almost indescribable 'magic' that pulses at the very core of the organisation. It makes their employees excited about clocking on.

From my first day at Nordstrom's twenty seven years ago, I knew I was part of something much bigger than myself, yet it was not daunting. I and the other employees knew we were being asked to be better human beings just by being associated with the firm and we knew it was not a hard task. It buoyed us along. It wasn't a job. It was an exciting part of our lives.

I've found the same at Walmart. The tide of customer focus pushes the employees along and they willingly get in the flow and enjoy the ride.

What's more important is that the customers enjoy the ride too and they return again and again to bring their friends with them.

So now it is your opportunity. Whether you feel your company is starting from scratch, or whether you, like all great companies, are committed to ongoing improvement, *Five Star Service on a One Star Budget* will fuel your journey. This is one book which you will want to share with your entire team.

Betsy Sanders
Author, "Fabled Service"
Founding Manager of Nordstrom, Southern California
Director of Wal-Mart Stores, Inc., Washington Mutual, Wolverine Worldwide, Wellpoint Health Systems, and Advantica Restaurant Group

Introduction

This book, like its older family member, *Make More Money from Every Sale*, is a do-it-yourself business manual designed to help you with three things:

1. You'll get motivation to continue doing the things that matter – whether you are at this time struggling or blessed with untold success.

2. You'll find this is a good way to stand back from your business and assess its condition and then work on it.

3. You'll have the tools in your hand to guide your team members toward brilliant customer service.

You have a manual here which duplicates the kind of work I've been doing in companies for twenty years and which might have cost them thousands of dollars in consulting and training fees. It will cost you much less, yet if you do the exercises and share them with your customer service team you could get thousands of dollars of value from it.

One baker in a country town has banked $150,000 extra this year because he did everything I wrote about in the first book. I tell you this because you might not understand the value of what you now hold in your hands. If you received it as a gift it is easy to say, 'Huh! A book' and to take it home and put it by the bed as a 'get-around-to-reading' job one day.

It is something you should read and then come back to time and again. With *Make More Money...* managers would put a sticky note in a chapter and hand it to a team member before work or before a team meeting and ask the team member to lead a discussion based on the main thought in the lesson.

It also serves as a good hiring tool. Ask potential employees whether they are willing to adhere to the lessons in the book before starting them on the job.

I'm hoping by reading this book you'll raise the standards for all of us, and make the rest of us wish we were just like you.

SECTION 1

You CAN give five star service on a one star budget

It doesn't take money or genius or qualifications or congenial circumstances to give five star service. It just takes 'heart'.

LESSON 1

The Five Star Man

A job as a doorman at an hotel would appear to be a mundane, unrewarding, mindless occupation; unloading bags, calling cabs, giving directions, parking cars and delivering parcels – all while torturing your feet standing in the rain or the blazing hot sun.

Had dinner? Try the fish!

There's at least one man who has turned the job into a daily star-studded performance. His name is Ric Angeletti and he works at the Hindley Park Royal in Adelaide, South Australia.

Try the fish!

Ric thinks he's in show business. When he sees your car or cab pull up, he runs over to your trunk and waves at you through the window with a cheeky grin.

Before you've turned off the ignition, he's unloaded your bags and opened your door.

'Park here for now and we'll shift your car later', he says with a wink. 'The parking inspector is my cousin.'

'Had dinner? Try the fish! My other cousin Louie caught it this morning.' He imitates Louie reeling in a big one. Then he adds, 'It dropped off the fish truck'.

He's laughing. You're laughing. You're glad you've booked into this hotel already.

He has a different packet of mindless, cheerful prattle for everyone, regardless of whether you are the State Premier, the chairman of a major corporation, or a couple of country bumpkin honeymooners. He can hold four conversations at once, manage three couples' bags and hail two cabs all without his feet touching the ground, or breaking his precious smile – all day.

He knows every restaurant in town, every employee in the hotel, all the cab drivers in the street, and half the passers-by.

He can remember names better than the tax department, and his recall on faces is astounding.

When he recognises me he shouts playful abuse from the doorway. He pities all the friends I take there for their bad luck in being with me and has enormous mock compassion for my wife.

Poor Darling. You should have married a doorman.

'Get Ric!'

After Adelaide lost the Formula I Grand Prix to Melbourne, the Williams motor racing team was asked where they would like to stay in the city, having enjoyed the Park Royal's hospitality for ten years. Their reply was straight from the hip. 'Who cares', they shrugged, 'as long as Ric Angeletti is there.'

Everyone knows him. Everyone is proud of him. His employer told me, *'He's one of a kind.* His consistency is the thing that amazes us all the most. If he ever has a bad day, you'd never know it. He's happy all the time. We call him our Hotel Ambassador. He's ours and we tell everyone else, "Hands off"! '

Countless awards

Ric has been given countless awards including the keys to the City of Adelaide, and he's been honoured as South Australian of the Year – a title shared with sports stars, scientists and philanthropists. Not bad for being a 'common doorman'.

Whether Ric worked at a five star hotel or a moonlit doss house he would take his five star service with him.

Why?

That's a good question and you'll find the answer in this book as you invest a couple of valuable hours thinking seriously about the level and quality of service you are offering in your business. *It doesn't matter whether you are the owner or 'one of the workers'; it doesn't matter whether you work in a one-person booth or a major national department store;* it doesn't matter whether you have a zillion dollar support budget or you are flat stony broke; it doesn't matter whether your customers are nice or nuts. You'll be challenged to lift your game, rouse yourself, catch a vision, lift your sights and discover that you too can give five star service on a one star budget.

FIVE STAR IDEA:
Whether you're the CEO or the cleaner – even the door person – open your mind and ask if there is the slightest possibility that you could find a way you can turn your job into an all-singing, all-dancing, star-studded, thrill-a-minute performance?

Footnote: I just read this chapter to the housemaid cleaning my room who wanted to know what I was typing. I read her the first chapter. When I finished reading the Five Star Idea she snorted, 'In a housemaid's job? Not likely!'

I thought straight away of the gorgeous smiling face of Becca, the housemaid in the Regent Hotel in Fiji.

She called on all the rooms at the end of her shift to see if her guests were happy with the little things she had done for them that day – always something different – such as lining up their toiletries and cosmetics like soldiers, or draping their jewellery over the mirror, or laying out their coins in a circle, or folding their cast off shirts, or rolling up their socks in their shoes. She expected no tip. She begged no recognition. She just wanted to share fresh Fijian hospitality and to make sure we felt at home.

Becca had decided to make every day a performance.

LESSON 2

Get Your Heart Right

Tense up! We're rolling.

No Warning

> Bob Phillips was the floor manager at Channel Seven in Adelaide when I performed in a pre-school show called, *Ready. Set. Go!*
>
> He had a warped way to manage the on-camera talent. Instead of preparing us for a 'take' with encouragements like, 'Nice and relaxed now', or 'Ready to roll', or 'We're going for a take', or even plain old 'Stand by!' Bob would bark with a provocative grin and no warning, 'Tense up! We're rolling'.

Big picture stuff

It was our wake-up call to throw body and soul into every show and think about nothing else but the audience. He didn't really want us to be tense. It was just Bob's way of teasingly reminding us of the responsibility of broadcasting. It wasn't about getting through to lunch time, or to the next coffee

Tense up! We're rolling.

break or getting paid on Tuesday. It was about the little viewers at home sitting there in their pyjamas eating their toast, big eyes open wide, fresh pudgy faces full of wonder and joy, singing when we sang, clapping when we clapped and jumping when we jumped.

Bob made us focus past the cynical all-male adult crew who would have preferred to work the Footy Show roster. He made us see the big picture. He reminded us that it wasn't only a job. He reminded us that it was really important to someone out there even if he or she were only three years old.

It was like reminding us of that special 'something' Ric Angeletti possesses.

You're on centre stage now

This book is saying, 'Tense up. We're rolling!'

The show has started. The store is open. The people are coming in. They have money in their purses and they won't be happy until it's all spent on good value products and services.

Smile. You're on camera. Dance. You're on stage. Sing. Tape is rolling. You're in front of the microphone. Strut your stuff lady. Do your thing fella. And give it all you've got. *Get out that special magic that is you at your best.*

It used to be called 'heart'.

Tom Peters now calls it your 'other'.

What's your 'other'

Excellence isn't good enough

In *The Tom Peters Seminar* (Random House, New York, 1994) he says excellence is no longer enough. On tour in 1996 with my friend and fellow speaker Alan Patching he confided that some of the top companies he wrote about in 1984 in his book, *'In Search of Excellence'* are out of business.

'Why?' asked Alan.

'They stopped at excellence', Peters replied.

In other words they didn't explore their heart – their 'other'.

What's 'other'?

You can't touch it but it's there

It's what Phillip Morris got when they bought Kraft for $12.9bn, and they could only account for $1.3bn worth of stock, plant and machinery. They had bought $11.6bn worth of 'other'– ingenuity, creativity, belief, drive, passion and flair. It's what made Apple owners jeer the revelation that Bill Gates had bought into Apple in 1997. They had become what Apple's marketing guru Guy Kowasaki calls 'raging inexorable thundering evangelists' for Apple. True believers in Apple's 'other', they wanted Apple to survive on its own. It's what Lee Iacoca put back into Chrysler. It's what Michael Eisner put back into Disney.

Only one box of cheese left, but cheer up. You've got me and the boys!

Your 'other' is your intellect, your passion, your imagination; the 'vibe' and the 'feel' over your organisation and your part in it. It's your magnetism with which you can repel or attract. Every organisation and every person has 'other'. It can be positive or negative, nice or nasty, good or bad, hot or cold; it can be obvious, it can stick out like a sore thumb, it can stand out like a beacon or it can be neutral, unnoticeable, hard to pick and vague. But *it can never be non-existent.*

Some people give out a feeling as if something cold and damp were slithering over your chest while you were asleep. Others give you the same feeling you'd get if you were standing next to Kieren Perkins when he got out of the pool in Atlanta, after he won the gold medal in the 1500 metres in 1996. Do you remember it? His was the innocent charisma of the ecstatic champion – the same irrepressible joy Cuba Gooding Jr. showed when he won the Oscar for his supporting role in the movie, Jerry Maguire.

Care or care not. There is no pretend

This book is about your 'other'. You've got 'other' whether you like the idea or not. It is so important that you understand this. Customer service is not something you can fake. You either care or you don't. In the movie 'The Empire Strikes Back', Yoda, the last of the Jedi knights says to his young disciple, Luke Skywalker, *'Do, or do not. There is no try.'* There is no half measure or getting 'close enough' with customer service. There is no pretending you care.

Care or care not. There is no pretend
And if you care not then please do the rest of us a favour and go away.

You can't just go through the motions of customer service and hope to get away with it. It's no use pasting on a half-baked smile because the sign in the staff bathroom tells you to. It's valueless approaching customers in a damp rag kind of way saying, 'Ya right there?' just because the staff memo asks you to acknowledge shoppers. It's in or out. If your heart is not in it, get another job. As my friend John Smart says, 'Stay home and be happy'.

If your 'other' is right, the rest is easy

If you think your job is an opportunity to perform for the customers and to take centre stage every day, that's your 'other'. You'll glow with it like Moses coming down from Mount Sinai. You'll find this book a treasure chest of precious gems and priceless jewellery. You'll love it and I'll feel like I'm preaching to the choir.

If you think your job is just a means to get money, that in turn is your 'other'. It will stick out all over you like echidna quills. You'll find this book annoying and superficial.

So the question is: What is your 'other' and what's it worth?

FIVE STAR IDEA:
Make a comparison of two lists:
List One: Write down the elements of the 'other' that you bring to your organisation.
List Two: Ask a few people what they think you bring to the organisation by way of 'other'.

If you are using this book as a seminar manual, break into groups and get your colleagues to tell you what your 'other' is.

LESSON 3

Is the customer always right?

Who started this idea that the customer is always right?

Back in the bad old days

Do you remember watching a movie or TV 'western' which featured a general store?

Little House on the Prairie had one and so did *Dr Quinn, Medicine Woman.* Those store owners seemed to run the town. They were downright ornery too. They treated their customers like second rate human beings and put their own opinions about everything out to air in the street. They thought they knew a lot about life because they owned a store but their ignorance on most topics was always a highlight of the shows.

They saw their customers as adversaries.

They portrayed the idea that the customer was always wrong and furthermore that the customers should consider themselves lucky to even have their wonderful store in their town.

'Them fools down in Washington don't know what they're a-doin'. Some feller called Lincoln says he's gonna free the slaves. As if that would catch on.'

Wasn't that Horace Van der Gelder's view of life as depicted in 'Hello Dolly'? Younkers was one lucky town because he lived in it and granted the citizens the opportunity to sample his wares. Note they were 'his'. He was a mean old 'tight wad'.

If these shopkeepers thought you were unworthy of owning a certain item, they would tell you to your face that you had no right buying it. If you were overdue with your credit they announced to a shop full of your neighbours that you were dishonest or poor.

I grew up in a neighbourhood like that

Unfortunately these adversarial attitudes lasted through the decades into the fifties and sixties where I grew up and sadly they still exist today, even in some of the most glamorous shopping centres in the world.

> As I recall, nearly every shopkeeper in my neighbourhood in the fifties had a nasty relationship with his or her customers.
>
> You took your life in your hands if you called in on the butcher at five o'clock and asked for sixpence worth of minced meat for your kitten.
>
> 'You don't give my minced meat to cats.'
>
> You trembled as you took your threepence to the lolly shop and asked for a 'hapenee's' (halfpenny's) worth of bullets and a penny's worth of honey bears and then another 'hapenee's' worth of bullets, and a penny's worth of raspberries.
>
> 'Make up your mind before you get here!'
>
> And angels protect you if you went to the barber with wavy hair.
>
> 'Look at this lads. A girl in a barber's shop. Let's get rid of her curly bits so she doesn't look like such a sissy!'
>
> The green grocer swore at you.

> The draper was a pig.
>
> The postmaster always made it look like he was in pain when he got out of his chair to sell you a stamp and complained that you didn't have the right money.
>
> It was horrible. My mother's words, 'Run up to the shop' still make me shiver.
>
> I often ask myself how have I ended up spending my life being so nice to retailers with my seminars, books, tapes and Internet sites?
>
> It's a wonder I survived.
>
> It's no wonder they didn't.
>
> They blamed the big shopping centres.
>
> I'm sure they were right.

A couple stood out. The Robins boys used to call on Thursdays with the home delivery in a big pine fruit crate and unload everything on the kitchen table for Mum. They whistled.

Fred Harris always smiled as he hobbled to the counter with his bung leg. He always said, 'Hello boys'. You'd buy something and feel like you had to stop and say something nice to him. Everyone liked Fred. He'd let you sit out on his porch in his garden seat to drink your Williams Icy.

But he was the exception rather than the rule.

Isolation gave them licence

I've no doubt that the characters portrayed in those western shows were caricatures of real life in the last century. Business in the tiny towns was hard work and they figured that customers only made it harder and for that they were to be punished with abuse, bad temper and poor service. Picture it: A one-store town with the next town fifty or more miles away and most of the citizens restricted to travelling on Shanks' Pony or fighting a mule all the way there and back – no consumer affairs departments, no complaints tribunal, and no competition.

Did you put up with the poor treatment? What else could you do?

Something had to change

It was against this background that the groundbreaking emporiums built their extraordinary customer-first empires. Establishments like Marshall Field's in Chicago, Macey's in New York, Harrods in London, Galeries Lafayette in Paris, David Jones in Sydney, and Myer in Melbourne built their fortunes on slogans like these:

> *Give the lady what she wants*
> *If you can't find it, we'll get it for you*
> *No request too small*
> *Not happy with it? We'll exchange it*
> *Every purchase covered by our no-questions-asked refund policy*
> *and the big one...*
> *In our stores the customer is always right*

The owners fostered these attitudes because their employees had only been exposed to the gruff behaviour of the general storekeepers of the day in the small towns and local neighbourhoods. Employees needed re-programming. Their attitudes needed reshaping. There was no way the small town mentality (I'm right. You're wrong!) would serve a store in a big city where competition abounded. Offended customers could simply walk next door. In time they could catch a tram to the next block, a train to the next town and it would not be long before they could drive their own car to the next big city.

An unfortunate legacy

One of those slogans has backfired. The one that causes retailers the most grief is the one about the customer being right.

I meet retailers who are so frustrated by that statement.

You sold me the wrong dress size!

• There you stand with a customer swearing that the sweater they bought last week was one size but by the time they got it home and put it on their child the garment had changed size. You want to tell the customer that it couldn't possibly have happened but you know from the slogan that the customer is always right. You just can't bring yourself to say how sorry you are for stocking such rubbish.

• How about the situation where you warned the customer not to freeze the garlic bread because it was best eaten fresh but they did it anyway and now here they are telling you that you make lousy garlic bread. You want to tell them they are stupid but then you remember that the customer is always right. The words stick in your throat and you just can't apologise for being a lousy baker.

• And then there's the day that a customer pops in unannounced and wants their hair done right away declaring that she has an appointment this time every month. You know she is wrong and yet you know you are supposed to say she is right. You split in half, dumbfounded at the idea.

And what about a thousand other instances where the customer is just plain outright clear-as-day – W.R.O.N.G.? How can you go along with 'The customer is always right'?

Let me get you off the hook.

Erase that slogan from the memory banks and replace it with

'The customer is always first'

or for those who like to split hairs and ascribe to the view that their sales team members are always first,

'The customer is a top priority'.

You need neither agree nor disagree with the customer who is wrong.

You can in fact ignore the whole topic. This kind of thinking lets you focus on the solution. Who is right or who is wrong is no longer important. Your suggestion about settling the matter becomes the only issue in your mind so you keep this customer's money coming into your store.

FIVE STAR IDEA:
Worry less about who is right and who is wrong. Just get the problem fixed.

LESSON 4

It isn't hard to be better. Not many people are doing it

I will never forget the first time I heard a motivational speaker. I had grown up listening to great preachers, teachers and storytellers and they were the only model I had for my interest in speaking, but on that night in February 1978 I heard the founder of the National Speakers Association of Australia, John Nevin, give his 'Mountain Man' presentation and I finally knew what I wanted to be when I grew up. I was already thirty years old.

He made one thing clear. *You don't have to be that much better than the rest to be better than the rest.*

We breed 'em to win.

John pointed out through his interest in horse racing that most of the great prize winners did not win the big stakes by much more than a head or even a nose. I'd never thought about it like that. I guess I had grown up believing that the winners in life were all miles ahead of the pack. They were somehow luckier or more gifted. I, being the third son of a poor widow from an average neighbourhood was never likely to enjoy such 'luck'.

But he told us that great golfers only won major tournaments by one putt. He showed us that the difference between a pass and a fail, or an 'A' and a 'B' was often only one mark.

The great tennis champions only hit the ball over the net one more time than the people they defeat. Many football games and hockey matches are won by only one goal – just a flick or a kick or a nudge of the ball a couple of degrees either way will make the difference between the championship and relegation.

> It made me think of Victor Borge's story about the man who invented a new soft drink. He started with a drink called '1Up' but after meeting with no success he went on to invent '2Up', then '3Up', each time without success. He continued on all the way to '6Up' finally dying in despair, a broken failure.
> 'But', shouts Borge, 'He don't know how close he got!'

I took John Nevin's message to heart and have made it part of my own. It was the way I brought up my four children. I told them they didn't have to be brilliant. They just had to give life a good shot and it would make a huge difference because so many other kids and their parents couldn't give a darn. They would stand out in a crowd all their lives because for most people even being average is an effort but being a bit above average is not an impossible ask.
I speak to a lot of retailers in my work. Most of them are wonderful conscientious people. Others wouldn't work in an iron lung. Sometimes I think I am wasting my life talking to people who will never get it. Five Star Service is so easy to provide but too many lazy self-interested sods can't see it.

However this makes it so much easier for the rest of us. We only have to do a little better than them and we will stand out like well lit cities on a hill.

Activity

Part 1. Take twenty minutes and go mystery shopping in stores where you are not known. This exercise alone is worth a thousand times the price of this book.

During retail training sessions I send guests on these assignments often. I ask them to look for the following:

Do the store people notice you?

Do they make eye contact?

If they greet you what do they say?

How long does it take them to approach you?

Do they ask you a question about your needs?

Do they make a suggestion and tell you a benefit of the product or do they rabbit on about its features?

Did they make you feel like buying?

What is your assessment?

When they report back I ask them why they think retailers are having a hard time. In one accord they shout in exasperated self-condemnation, 'Because we are idiots'.

'They don't even look up from their book work.'

'They natter amongst each other.'

'One guy handed us a card as we walked in the door and said, "Here's the boss's card. He's away today but he's the best one to talk to about discounts".'

I've done this hundreds of times and collected a mine of independent impressions. I'm sad to say that although I wouldn't agree about the 'idiot' label, I have had to come to this conclusion: Retailers are not very good at the customer interface aspect of their business. If you can fix this alone you will work miracles on your bank balance.

Part 2. List all the simple things you can do better as a result of seeing others in action.
eg Smile more, keep stock neat, sound chirpy,

____

____

____

____

____

____

FIVE STAR IDEA:
Look around you at the other retailers nearby and become convinced about how easy it is to be better simply because they are not putting in the effort. You CAN give Five Star Service.

LESSON 5

THE FIVE STAR RETAILER

There are sales people and there are shop assistants

There are shop assistants

Some retail employees only start thinking about their job when they walk in the door, stop thinking about it when they walk out and think as little about it as possible in between. They take their Shop Assistant's Industrial Award literally. They assist the shop.

They open it, staff it, mind it, tidy it, tend it, 'man' it, and close it.

They confuse themselves with the shop counter

They count the hours until home time, calculate the days until their day off, compute whether their money will last until pay day, and estimate the weeks until their holidays. They count the number of good-looking passers-by, the flies in the window, the phone interruptions, and the number of silly customers.

They'd be happier if nobody came in and messed up their displays or fiddled with the stock.

They might be very nice people but in a business they are as effective as a one – armed archer.

And then there are salespeople – Show biz people

But when you meet a real salesperson you see the difference straight off. I saw one at Barmera, a little tourist and farming town at Lake Bonney on the Murray River. It was in Barry and Blondie Wyman's B & B Fabrics and Fashions, a drapery store I came across while I was on a camping trip with my boys. Barmera has a population of four thousand five hundred and boasts about eighty-seven businesses. It's a really friendly place by the harshest judgement, but Barry stands out.

> When I walked in, one of the locals was harassing him for displaying outdated bowls hats and outfits in the store window. 'Disgusting', she was saying. 'The tourists will think Barmera's full of country bumpkins from the fifties.'
>
> He was responding with all the cheek in the world, 'They wouldn't fit you anyway, Mavis. Buy some towels while you're here to make it worthwhile dropping in.' She did.
>
> While he was sorting her out he was telling off another customer reminding her it was sale time and to put half her money back in her purse. She took out more.
>
> He came to me and saw my boys and me struggling to find a sun hat that fitted and which would also look 'cool'. He found them two brand name hats which cost more but told me if I bought them I could pick out a hat for myself for half price. I did.
>
> All the while he was taking credit cards, handling cash, throwing stock back on the pile and bagging up purchases for other customers.
>
> His hands were like a magician's. He carried sales dockets in his teeth. He had a pencil in his ear and a measuring tape around

his neck. 'To see how long you stand here without buying anything', he winked.

Everyone wore a wry smile at his antics and threw him answers to his off the cuff remarks from all over the store. He instinctively knew that there are still parts of retailing that can do with a huge dose of show business: in other words salesmanship.

Just wondered how long you'd been standing there.

Over the space of nine years he has built a reputation as an all-singing, all-dancing, all-laughing retail performer.

Does it work? Well you may ask.
To check my facts and figures about Barmera I called him a minute ago and he quietly let it drop that he had experienced a fifty-seven percent increase in his annual autumn sale this year. 'Business is still booming', he said. 'Must be the grape harvest!'

FIVE STAR IDEA:
It doesn't seem important where you are or what kind of market you're in. You can create five star service if you want to.
Put on a great show. Customers love it. And they'll come for miles just to watch you perform.

LESSON 6

Put Some Oomph in Your Ordinary!

You can create five star service if you want to – but you have to want to.

You have to give up your excuses first

Have you heard people say, 'But I just work in a shop. I'm an ordinary person in an ordinary shop selling ordinary products to ordinary customers. There's neither opportunity nor need for me to be a five star performer. And besides that, I'd feel silly being different from everyone else. There's nothing wrong with being ordinary.'

Perry Cross

I'm still recovering from meeting Perry Cross.

It was an awesome experience and it happened eighteen months ago.

A quadriplegic, still in his early twenties, he's the only university student on full life support. His wheel chair is fitted with a battery-operated ventilator. If the battery fails or his throat tube pops out, Perry's a goner! He moves the chair by controlling it with his chin and his plastic mouth tube. He has a team of twelve 'carers' who live with him in shifts, twenty-four hours a day – every day. They even sleep with him.

> At 19 he was fit, fast and fabulous. He was six feet four and was built like a bomb shelter. His life was sport, sport and more sport, and working in his parents' carpet retailing business.
> Then in a flash his life changed for good. He was trying out for the Gold Coast Under 19 rugby team and in a freak accident he suffered a broken neck.
> He says he knew instantly that his life as he'd known it was over. He couldn't move, couldn't feel and couldn't breathe.
> Two weeks later in hospital he discovered the weird sense of humour of other members of the 'club' as the other patients called their fellowship of immobility.
> One of the 'club members' asked him a totally distasteful riddle; The joke isn't important. Perry's conclusion is:
> 'What's the hardest thing about cooking vegetables?' asked the other patient. He paused and threw the punch line, 'Getting

their wheel chairs in the oven!'

Perry said to himself, 'You can't say a thing like that! That's shocking. But after I thought about it for a minute I realised, life wasn't so bad after all!'

Give me strength! 'Not so bad!' he says.

He'll be in that contraption totally dependent on others until he's an old man or until someone finds him a reversal process. Self pity is his undeniable right!

That's not how Perry sees it though.

'I've got so much potential' he says. 'There's so much I can do. There's so much I can achieve. I want to share that message with everyone.'

I felt like a fat forty-nine-year-old failure fooling around with my future and fussing about my frailties.

I took a deep breath of clean free air, all by myself, and decided to forge on.

FIVE STAR IDEA:
Go stand in front of a mirror and count your blessings one by one. Then as you look at your totally able body and ample opportunities, ask yourself, 'So what's your excuse? Why aren't you giving it all you've got?'

You are ten times better than you think you are.

LESSON 7

WHAT IS FIVE STAR SERVICE?

You already know about five star service

I'm not going to waste much printer's ink or many of God's good trees coming up with a definition for five star service. If I did it would read something like this and be really boring.

> Service is that value or quality surrounding the exchange of goods or services in a manner so as to be either pleasant or unpleasant depending on the attitude of the provider and the expectation of the recipient where one might at the same time and coinciding with the assessment determine a rating of stars as a measure of the perceived value of the service experienced whereby for example one star would be the grading given to service which could be seen as really stinking and two stars would be regarded as moderately stinking and... YAWN!

You already know what great service is and what it isn't.

How do good and bad service affect you?

Picture two occasions; one when you received five star service from a salesperson or service provider, and another when service was poor. You might need to scratch your head for the good one as most people tell me incidents like this are hard to recall because they are so rare. Let me help.

Was it at home, in a store, an hotel, or a restaurant?
Was it on holiday, during a break, on the weekend or during business hours?
At the time were you lost, lonely, bewildered, or scared?
Were you hungry, tired, flustered, or fed up?

Were you on your own, with family, with friends or in a crowd?
Were you trying to impress someone or please a companion or just getting some satisfaction for yourself?
Were you armed with cash, ready to decide, and pumped for a sale?

Think about the experience and reflect for a moment on three things:

1. What emotions did the positive experience evoke?
2. Recall the value of the goods or service around which the pleasurable experience was based.
3. Decide which aspect of the experience gave you the most pleasure – the thing or service itself or was it the behaviour of the person/s involved.

1. List the words which describe your feelings here.

For the good service	*For the bad service*
______________________	______________________
______________________	______________________
______________________	______________________

2. Write the value of the goods or services here.

Good service | *Bad service*

_______________ _______________

3. Write whether it was the goods or service provided or the service provider's behaviour which pleased you most.

Good service

❑ The service provider

❑ The product

Bad service

❑ The service provider

❑ The product

If you're taking this exercise as part of a group learning experience get someone to list the responses on a chart.

Now do the same kind of reflection again but this time focus on an experience where the service was 'B.A.D.' bad.

Compare your results

I've conducted this exercise for thousands of people in all walks of life and in a cross section of countries, viz: Australia, USA, New Zealand, Singapore, and the Philippines. I rarely find a variation. For twelve years I have kept records of their responses. Here are the most common responses. Are these like yours?

1. Most common words used to describe pleasant service experiences:

satisfied	delighted	excited
appreciated	amazed	wowed
contented	happy	pleased

needed	stunned	noticed
grateful	fabulous	wanted to come back
wanted to refer others	didn't want to go home	thrilled
comfortable	beautiful	enthusiastic
great	reassured	important

2. Most common words used to describe responses to unpleasant service experiences:

horrified	appalled	frightened
disgusted	vengeful	murderous
hateful	angry	furious
in a temper	dissatisfied	wanted to warn people
violent	fed up	mad
offended	sickened	shocked

3. And the value of the goods or services?

You would expect that emotions so exciting as listed first would have been aroused over goods and services valued at hundreds of thousands of dollars wouldn't you? You might even think that the people in the seminars were describing their feelings over winning an inheritance or finding a map for pirates' golden treasure buried in their back yard.

In fact the value for the pleasant experiences has ranged from 15¢ for a bit of cabbage to $125,000 for a house but the average value of the services as described to me over a dozen or so years has been an amazingly low $17.59.

You would also suspect that the value of the bad services which could bring out such horrific emotions and vengeance and blood lust would be in the millions. You would think that the people involved had had their villages bombed or their families kidnapped but the value here has been as low as 75¢ for a petrol cap to several hundred dollars for a bridal gown but with the average price only being $7.98.

4. Was it the goods and services which thrilled you or the manner of the person involved?

In a materialistic society and a 'things-happy' world you might think that the thousands of people in my seminars would have voted in favour of the 'thing' they purchased. On the contrary, an overwhelming eighty-four percent (84%) of cases have cited the attitude and behaviour of the service provider as being the cause of the positive or negative emotions aroused.

The guy was real sharp.

Five Star Service is self explanatory. It needs no defence and little explanation. It also seems to need minimal expenditure if any. It appears as though it CAN be provided on a one star budget.

FIVE STAR IDEA:
Make it a goal – no, a passion – to create that list of positive emotions in all your customers.

LESSON 8

CHECK YOUR A.S.S.E.T.S.

Bet you've never thought of this...

Your best assets are not your stock, or your plant, or your equipment, or your proprietary name, or your trade marks, or your uniforms, or even the goodwill in your business.

Your best assets are your intangibles: Your dreams, your drive, your passion, your willingness to work, your eagerness to create opportunities for others. If your business fell over tomorrow you'd still have them all. You'd have lost nothing real and you could start again with everything that is permanent. The rest is only stuff. That's why so many wealthy people can say they have been broke plenty of times in their lives. They might have lost their physical assets on a number of occasions but their hearts were unfazed.

They don't work like other assets which you keep

These A.S.S.E.T.S. cost you nothing to acquire and cost you nothing to use. They belong to that strange group of commodities whereby you get more of them by giving away what you already have.

In any publication on customer service you will find a chapter or two dedicated to what is sarcastically called smile training. This book has only one, so pay attention while I do it justice. You can address this section every day by saying , 'Check your A.S.S.E.T.S.', to each other any time you think the team needs a lift. It will put you out in front of everyone in your shopping centre.

A – Appearance

We scan you from head to toe and notice your face, your hair, your shoes and your torso and decide whether we like you. Then we decide whether we can trust you just by the look of you. I know people shouldn't judge a book by its cover but if they didn't why would their mothers have needed to tell them for the last four thousand years not to judge a book by its cover.

Check these assets: (the first two are unarguable. The others are opinions – good opinions mind you, tried and tested by the most successful retailers.)

• **Clean hands.** People in businesses where there is heavy or grubby equipment often pass over customers' products or receipts looking like they have been giving a manual enema to a dead wombat that's been on a blackberry diet. There are stacks of good industrial cleaners that are great for your skin and don't need water. Gloves are cheap too.

I still see people in food stores politely cough into their hand to stop spreading germs and then continue to make a sandwich. Yeee- uck!

• **No gum chewing or cigarette smoking – or food or drink in sight.** This is mandatory in the food industry. In other businesses I still see receptionists and sales team members with lunch at their desk or half finished coffee on their counters while customers approach. Team members are allowed refreshment so managers need to establish rules which are both fair and at the same time give a snappy impression to customers.

• **Neat hair** – combed, brushed or tied back – not hanging over your face like a seductive sweaty model in a tropical photo; not in a green spike unless you work in a boutique environment where you are supposed to draw attention to yourself as an exhibit of what the establishment can do.

• **Tucked in shirt or blouse** with a neat waist. Even if you are of a more ample figure you can still be tucked in.

• **Tie or scarf tied straight.** A neat neckline highlights your face.

• **Clean shoes.** People with boots think they have to keep them scuffed to look cool. Be different. Make yours shine. My dad was a tyre fitter yet he went to work in a suit and gold cuff links and changed when he got there. He shone his shoes so he could see his face in them.

• **Socks up.** Nothing looks more sloppy than socks at half mast.

• **Name tags.** Would someone please tell the designers of uniforms that the names need to go on the right side? Most people are right handed. They approach customers favouring their right side. If

If a job's worth doing it's worth dressing up for.

they have to shake hands they do it right side out. When the name tag is on the left side it is nearly always out of view and therefore useless. By the time customers have finished leaning around to your left to read your name you think they want to dance with you.

Oh yes! Let's make names one centimetre high in lower case (half an inch) and in a contrasting colour – and first name only. We don't want your life history – just an identification so we know who you are for next time.

And those name bars with the horizontal pin? They always point to the ground. Chuck 'em.

Activity:
Get your team to do a self assessment on their own appearance and then ask them to assess each other. Include yourself. This might come as a shock to some people but just remind them that their job isn't about them – it's about their customers and that you will not tolerate anything that prevents customers from getting the value they need from owning your products.

S – Smile
Want to be really different? Want to stand out from every other retailer in your centre or strip? It's easy. Smile all day.

I conducted a survey for a shopping centre and sent mystery shoppers out to do a head count on the retailers who were smiling. They had to be counted whether they were with customers or not. How many do you estimate they found?

I thought they might find fifty percent.

They found none. Out of two hundred stores they found no-one smiling. Isn't that something? And these dopey people wonder why retailing is suffering a battering. At the same time they're blaming their landlords for not making the centres attractive enough.

Kevin Marks, the State Manager for Bob Jane T-Marts was holidaying with his wife in Sydney and strolling around a popular tourist spot. He meandered into a refreshment shop for a drink. The operator was cleaning the fridge door glass with his sleeve and a bit of breath fog.

Kevin 'hrrmfed' to get the chap's attention, who without looking at him said,

'Be with you in a tick'.

'While you're there at the fridge I'll have a couple of orange juices thanks', said Kevin.

The operator finished cleaning the glass, grabbed two bottles of juice and plonked them on the counter.

'Three dollars!'

Kevin handed over the money and like me, being a little on the provocative side, he said,

'I suppose a smile is out of the question'.

'Oh Yeah. And where are you from?'

> 'Adelaide.'
>
> 'Typical!' he sneered. 'All the smart alecs come from Adelaide!'

Welcome to the city of the Olympic Games!

I don't know what you can do other than remind yourself all day to think happy thoughts.

Such as?

Be glad you can eat three times a day – even five or six times if you're so inclined. Billions can't.
Be glad you have shelter. Billions don't.
Be glad you sleep in a bed. Billions don't.
Be glad you have the dignity of work – a job and an income. Billions don't.
Be glad you live in a free country. Billions don't.
Be glad you can vote for whomever you choose. Billions can't.
Be glad you can read. Billions can't.
Be glad you have had a great education. Billions haven't.
Be glad you have running water at home and don't have to walk five miles to get it from a polluted well. Billions have to.
Be glad you can go out at night relatively safely. Billions can't.
Be glad that if you get sick, the longest you have to wait for hospitalisation is a couple of days. Billions just curl up and die.

Get the picture? If we took away only one of those things you'd have plenty to scowl about. But you've got them all and more. Couldn't you just give us a nice happy face?

Activity:

Agree as a team you will remind yourselves all day every day that
the dial needs a smile,
the face needs some grace,
the moosh needs a push,
the kisser needs a blisser,
the countenance needs some maintenance
the mask needs to bask
the visage needs a massage and
the make-up needs a shake up

S – Sound happy to help

Give these sloppy approaches the axe.

Ya right there?
Are you OK?
Can I help you?
Yes?
Next!
Who's next?
Want something?
Ya being served?
Just the cabbage?
Try sounding like a fellow human being.

Try saying,
Hello.
Good morning. I'll be here if you need me.

Hello. I'm Colin. Have you been here before?
Hello. If you have a question, I'll be over here. I'm Colin.

If you're in counter sales such as in food and drink, you could just try to sound bright and cheery and lead in with your prime product.

Hello. Can I fix you a coffee?
Hi there. Would you like some cake?

Instead of trying to look for gimmicks and tricks to stop shoppers from saying, 'No thanks. I'm just looking', just be so fabulous that perhaps they'll want to stop 'just looking' and ask for your help. And if they really are 'just looking', that's what they're doing and there's not a lot you can do about it.

Activity:
If you're reading this with your team, you need to stop here and brainstorm the best approaches to make it sound obvious that you are happy to help.

They may tell you this is a lot of hot air because so far everyone to whom they've said, 'Ya right?' has volunteered to buy something. Assure them that you could get a vending machine to do the same thing and that the vending machine would be cheaper to obtain and easier to maintain. The very people who claim we're treating them like robots are easiest to replace with a robot.

E - Enthusiasm

> 'Either this fellow is dead or my watch has stopped.'
> Groucho Marx

Walk through your shopping complex and look for enthusiastic retailers and you'll have to check your watch. You'd swear they've all been hit with a time delay spray.

No contest

As I type this I am looking up the word 'enthusiasm' in the word processor's thesaurus. Here's a list of words from the same side of the factory as enthusiasm:

ardour	fanaticism	ebullience
devotion	eagerness	excitement
verve	willingness	eccentricity
help	devotion	cooperation
intensity	obsessiveness	vitality

Do you think that's a bit much; a bit over the top? Perhaps you're scared of having this effect on people:

> I was once giving a lecture to a group of government employees (I call them 'employees' because I wouldn't want you to confuse them with 'workers'). As you can imagine, I was behaving as my normal low-key, genteel self. When they broke for coffee I overheard one woman say to her colleague, 'I need a pill. Mr Enthusiasm here gives me a headache.'

Perhaps this list appeals to you more. It's from the list of antonyms to enthusiasm.

calculation	calmness	caution

So far, not so bad, but read on...

carelessness	coldness	contempt
coolness	dejection	disaffection
doubt	dullness	indifference

A hot spring or a mud hole

See? There's no sitting on the fence. It's like this: Either you're enthusiastic or you're a waste of space. Either you're a hot spring or you're a mud hole. In beautiful Rotorua, New Zealand they have

They certainly don't rush their customers!

both. The hot springs they cap and harness. Their thermal energy is used to generate electricity to share light and power with many people. As for the mud holes, people avoid them because they stink and stick to your shoes. So are you a geyser or a mud hole?

Everything good comes from enthusiasm

My computer's resource file is full of slogans and quotes I've collected over many years. One look in the 'enthusiasm' entry tells me that enthusiasm is a key to success in any field of endeavour.

Which doctor?

If you had to undergo brain surgery and you had the choice of two equally skilled surgeons which of these two would you choose?

> Doctor Smiley, who says: I love this business. The human brain thrills me to my bones. I can't wait to see you well again. I'm going to do my best to find your problem and bring you through.
> Doctor Frownie, who says: This can be touch and go you know. It can be fatal if you're not careful. I'm always a little nervous fishing around inside something as important as a brain. You never know what you'll...

SLAM!

Yep. I'd run too. Doctor Smiley gets the vote even though he's no better qualified or skilled than Doctor Frownie.

Aim high

> Grandad Jim Cobbledick (a notorious skite) loved to tell about the day he took a short cut across the paddock where Murphy's bad-tempered bull grazed. He heard Murphy's bull coming for him at full tilt and he raced for the nearest tree with a low hanging branch

> about ten feet off the ground. He leapt for the branch for all he was worth but missed...
> Luckily he caught it on the way down.

That's enthusiasm! Aim higher than you need to – at everything.

T – Thankyou and Please

The Bulletin November 26, 1996, commented

> '... prison movies will never be the same if word leaks out about the new rules for warders at Port Lincoln in South Australia. They've been told to refer to the convicts as "clients" and address them as "Mr". Orders are to end with "Please".'

If they have to do it by legislation in prisons couldn't you do it by choice in your store?

Everything about you needs to say, 'Thank you for coming to my store. There are twenty other places you could spend your hard earned money but you've chosen my store to keep my business going and to keep me employed and my children fed. I appreciate the favour you've shown me.'

There is so much to be thankful for. How about this quaint old poem?

> The other day upon a bus,
> I saw a girl with golden hair.
> I envied her – she looked so gay –
> And wished I were so fair.

Then suddenly she rose to leave,
I watched her hobble down the aisle.
She had but one leg, and bore a crutch,
And as she passed – a smile.

Oh God forgive me when I whine –
I have two legs, the world is mine!

Later, I paused to buy some sweets.
The lad who sold them had such charm,
I stayed and talked to him a while,
If I were late, 'twould be no harm.
Then as I turned to leave he said,
'Thank you, you have been so kind,
I like to talk with folks like you –
You see – I'm blind'.

Oh God forgive me when I whine –
I have two eyes, the world is mine!

Still later passing down the street,
I saw a child with eyes of blue,
He stood and watched the others play,
It seemed he knew not what to do.
I stood a while and then I said
'Why don't you join the others, dear?'
He looked ahead without a word and then I knew
He could not hear.

> Oh God forgive me when I whine –
> I have two ears, the world is mine!
>
> Two legs to take me where I go,
> Two eyes to see the sunset's glow,
> Two ears to hear what I would know.
> Oh, God forgive me when I whine –
> I'm blessed indeed, the world is mine.

I'd like to hear more of this from retailers
Thanks for coming in
Please look around
Hello. Enjoy yourself while you're here
Welcome to Colly Pearce's
Have a great evening
I hope you enjoy that... (whatever they purchased)
Can I take your order please?
I'd love to serve you again
Please come back.

It's the same for the telephone

When you answer the telephone and the callers explain what they want say, 'Thank you for calling. I can help you with that. Can I ask you a couple of questions?' It's a bit different from the opposition who are just responding with, 'Right!'

And finish your calls with, 'Thanks for calling'.

S – Servant heart

I said most of this in Lesson 2.

A story will capture it again.

> Long ago, when the stars were still young, there lived an ageing desert king, rich in lands, livestock and gold. A widower, he had loved his wife dearly and desired for his son to enjoy the blessings of wedded joy such as he had known. When the time neared for his son to inherit the kingdom he desired greatly that his son marry wisely.
>
> To be a great king he knew that the prince should have a wife who would be loved by the people and who would become a worthy mother of a great nation. This would require no ordinary girl. As it was customary at the time for fathers to find their son a wife, he summoned his faithful servant and said, 'Go and find our distant relatives on the other side of the desert and select a wife worthy of my son and bring her here to take her place at his side'.
>
> As the servant set out with ten camels loaded with treasures for the future queen's dowry he said to himself, 'This is no easy task. What if I bring back the wrong girl? Should I choose her for her figure, her face or her family's fortune?'
>
> As he traversed the desert he formed a plan. When he reached the other side he found a well near the ancient family town and made his camels kneel down. He offered a prayer to the God of the king. 'This day I pray for success and for favour on my master...'
>
> Before he had finished his prayer he saw the most beautiful girl he had ever seen come near to draw water. He followed her and asked her for a drink, and she graciously lowered her water jar

for him. Then she told him to rest while she drew water for his camels. He watched her closely, not lifting a finger to help. She smiled at him and hummed softly, patting the camels' noses as she watered each one.

At the end of the task he called her to him and gave her a golden nose ring and two golden bracelets and asked to meet her family that he might offer her to his master's son to be a princess and queen.

She was both surprised and overjoyed and ran home to tell her mother.

How did he know to choose her?

The rest of his prayer still in his heart went like this, '...When the girls come out from the town to get water for their households and I ask one of them for a drink, have her offer to water my camels as well. Let her be the one.'

This babe's too good for the prince, Hal!

You see, each camel drank forty litres of water and her jar held only five litres; eight jars per camel. She would have had to make eighty trips to the well, and she did it cheerfully. The purpose of his prayer and of the task itself was to learn whether she was pretentious and proud and therefore an unworthy candidate for the royal household or whether she was humble and good at heart.

Faithfulness in the little servant acts is what sets champions apart. There have been times in my life when all I could do was keep grinding it out, 'same old same old', day after day, one foot up and one foot down, no glory, no gold, just serving. I wish I could add that I was serving cheerfully in all the cases. It was hard going, but I was at least serving. When people asked me how I was going I would have answered, 'Fourth camel, third jar!'

That's what a servant heart does.

I think you're getting the picture that being in business is not just about making a buck. You can see that operating for money alone is a shallow and pointless aim. You can't sustain it without providing a satisfying experience for your customers.

Don't be discouraged by the apparent success of lurk merchants. I've seen sharks and shonks make it for a while – even for a few years – on false promises and empty values, but in the end their evil deeds catch up with them and they fall over.

> Money gained by greedy means is a snare to its owner.
> The earnings of a faithful person feed generations.
> King Solomon the Wise

You already have the ability to use your A.S.S.E.T.S. You don't need a higher education or a training school to know what to do.

FIVE STAR IDEA:
Use this chapter as a pep up for your team once a week – even once a day.

SECTION 2

Why you DON'T give five star service on a one star budget

Thirteen reasons why you are not being written up in the leading business magazines for your stunning customer service and why customers aren't bringing back their friends by the bus load to do business with you.

LESSON 9

Reason #1 why you don't give five star service: You don't understand the purpose of being in business

Profit's OK

In the first book in this series, Make More Money from Every Sale I said that the purpose of business is two-fold: profit and service. If it's profit alone you have the purpose of the extortionists and the street gangs. If it's service alone then you have the purpose of St Vincent de Paul and the Salvos. Without service, you're a dressed up hoodlum; without profit you're a welfare worker.

In a book about service it is fitting that we spend a few moments thinking about profit.

Let's be clear about what this means.

• It doesn't mean charging higher than fair prices for commonplace goods and services.

• It doesn't mean that you make profit by paying employees, contractors and suppliers less than what is due to them or making them wait longer than they should for their payment.

• It doesn't mean that you make profit by following a policy of haste and greed, ripping out and destroying resources with no regard for the future and the people who will live in it.

• It doesn't mean ignoring the well-being of other people with whom we have business dealings.

But it does mean that if you don't run your business for profit you will not be in business for long. And it also means that with all the illegal and unscrupulous practices barred, the only way to make that profit is through providing five star service.

Business is a balance of service and profit.

Are you embarrassed?

Many business people start out in business to achieve all kinds of good. I am often surprised to see business people frowning on profit as if profit were somehow socially unacceptable. I hear them suggesting that they do not need a lot of money to get by and that profit is not their main motive. They give me the feeling that being in business is something to feel embarrassed about.

It is true that business and profit get bad press. Tonight I can almost guarantee that a television news show in your area will screen another example of how some horrible 'shonk' has exploited a widow or a senior citizen or an underprivileged person and made a cruel profit with disregard to principle and fair play.

It is no surprise to me that business people keep their business ambitions well hidden. Here is a list of the reasons people have given me for being in business.

- I want to show that it's possible to work in my chosen industry honestly and fairly
- I want to make a name for myself
- I want to leave my mark
- I want to leave my kids something to go on with
- I want to serve the poor with my wealth
- I want to give the unemployed a chance
- My partner and I wanted to do something together
- I want to help young people get a start
- I want to restore faith in the retired worker
- I want my business to spread the awareness of Greenpeace,

    (or save the whales,
    or food for the hungry,
    or non violent homes,
    or the Gospel,
    or family values,
    or good reading habits,
    or the rights of indigenous people
    housing for street people,

or eight hundred and fifty-four thousand other well-intentioned notions and ideals)

They use cover up language such as,

- I work for myself
- I work from home
- I have a practice (I love the way medical people are never in business)
- I have a professional consultancy
- I'm a subcontractor
- I work in my husband's business
- I'm in manufacturing
- I've set up by myself

They are struggling against the reality of business. They think business is about their personal freedom, working their own hours, not answering to a boss, leasing a car in their business name, or being free of office politics.

It's not. It's about helping customers to help you make a buck.

Regardless of your enterprise, if you do not have profit as your prime purpose you will no longer be in business and you will not be able to do the good that you set out to do.

FIVE STAR IDEA:
Get out your highlighter and underline this sentence. The purpose of business is to make a profit by providing fabulous five star service!

LESSON 10

Reason #2 why you don't give five star service: You don't understand customers

Quick summary

If you can't be bothered reading the rest of the lesson I'll give you the bottom line:

> Customers are totally taken up with their own importance.
> Work with this and you'll be happy.
> Fight it and you'll be miserable.

Potted history of modern psychology

Human beings – homo sapiens – our customers – built a little lower than the angels and a little taller than the grass – the pinnacle of creation – the highest form of life – students of the stars – are the most blessed of all creatures great and small. Shakespeare (*Hamlet*, II,ii) described us this way,

> What a piece of work is man!
> How noble in reason! how infinite in faculty!
> in form, in moving, how express and admirable!
> in action how like an angel! in apprehension how like a god!
> the beauty of the world! the paragon of animals!

You'd think we could be better customers wouldn't you?

Thinkers have been trying to unravel the riddle of why customers behave the way they do for thousands of years. I can't solve the riddle myself, nor can I pretend to have read all the studies in Western philosophy, but I have noticed a trend and I'll share it with you.

The Greeks and self-happiness

Alexander the Great's teacher, the all-wise Aristotle, believed that the goal of human beings is happiness. Happiness is the fruit of fulfilling a function, he argued, and to Aristotle the human being is 'the rational animal' whose function is to reason. For Aristotle the happy life is the life governed by reason.

Aristotle's philosophy has affected Western thought about the nature of humanity like no other. Didn't he write the song, *Don't Worry! Be Happy!*

The Church and self-love

The church has consistently portrayed the view that humans are unhappy because they are rotten sinners. And what is a sinner? Basically it's someone who loves him/herself more than God or his/her fellow humans. It's someone who breaks any of the ten commandments best summed up by the admonition, *Love God and love your neighbour — as much as you love yourself.*

The Good Book makes it clear that just as we need a law to remind us not to speed in our car, we are so prone to self interest that we need a law – commandment – direct orders – to love God and other people. Apparently we can arrive at one destination in the dark without directions but the other needs flashing road signs.

Descartes and self -awareness : 'I'm here, so there!'

Back around 1620 AD the French Grand Daddy of modern philosophy, Rene Descartes came up with the first lesson for Philosophy 101, *I think. Therefore I am.* Basically it means that when you think, you not only think but you are also aware of thinking and therefore you know you exist. (I find stepping bare foot on a bindii has the same effect.)

He'd be proud of me because the primary aim of his school of philosophy was to analyse complex ideas into simpler ones and that's what I'm doing here. Are you getting it? Descartes started with the spotlight centre stage focused on 'I'.

Adler and self-significance

Missing a few centuries we bump into Alfred Adler the Austrian (1870-1937) who espoused the view that human activity is motivated by striving from a feeling of inferiority toward superiority and perfection. Everyone feels inferior and in a lifelong drive for power we follow our own unique set of goals.

He told us that we are born with a governing mechanism called *social interest* which enables us to relate to other people and to place the good of society above self interest.

He had obviously not been to the historic Adelaide Crows back-to-back Aussie Rules Grand Final victory with my mates Wally and Helen. Seems to me that football fans' social interest gland could do with a bit of oiling.

There's a thread

A couple of threads are emerging. One is that the old 'Homo Sapio Customos' are complex little blighters and the other is that they are inordinately fascinated with themselves.

Freud and self-satisfaction

Most people in the West today observe human behaviour in Freudian terms. Although he has his detractors, he greatly advanced the field of psychiatry and his work has helped millions of mentally ill people. (You've noticed how many of them have become your customers as part of their recovery therapy.)

He determined that each person is born with biological instincts such as the drive for sexual satisfaction and the drive to satisfy hunger. He called the mental representation of these instincts the *id.* The *ego* is the part of our minds that helps us distinguish between desire and reality. For most of us the drives remain hidden, but balanced by what Freud called the *superego*, the governor of moral behaviour. Sometimes the parts conflict and that's when you are faced with customers in psychological disturbance – their instincts override their sense of equilibrium.

It's a bit like the rat and the foot pedal experiment.

> Although I have never tried it, I am told that you can sticky tape a wire to the sexual pleasure centre of a rat's brain and close the circuit by wiring the other end through a battery to one of two foot pedals. One foot pedal releases a pellet of yummy rat food and the other foot pedal releases an electric current that sets off a sensation of sexual pleasure for the rat*.

> After sampling the two pedals the rat quickly learns which one gives him more jollies than the other and over a few days he blisses himself to an exhausting but smiling demise.
>
> * For foot pedal orders including fitting instructions see catalogue at end of book.

That would be one psychologically disturbed rodent.

Freud tells us that we are driven by basic self oriented pleasures which can sometimes get out of balance.

Maslow and self-fulfilment

Abraham Harold Maslow (1908-1970) is the hinge on which the gate of psychological studies swing. He said that we are controlled by our choices and our values, not as the others thought, by our environment or by unconscious drives. He says we are awake to our motives all the time.

He said we respond to a package of needs, whereby we must fulfil the most basic ones before we can satisfy the next levels.

His so-called hierarchy of needs looks like this:

Level 1 The need for food and shelter.

Level 2 The need for safety.

Level 3 The need for love and belonging.

Level 4 The need for self esteem.

Level 5 The need for fulfilling one's unique potential – or self actualisation.

Can you see that when a customer meets you in your store, you are confronted by one mesmerising mass of molecules and mystery? Your customer isn't just looking for a dress. Your customer may be looking to satisfy any one of Maslow's needs – even more than one.

Sure she wants to protect herself against the cold south wind but if that is all she wants, a chaff bag will do the job perfectly. There's more to dress choosing than Level One needs. She wants to attract someone to love and belong to, she wants to look 'nice', and she wants to be known as someone with taste.

You'll do better when you stop to think about why a customer might be shopping with you.

General trends

Today there seem to be more and more scientists concluding that the prime drive for everyone is the need for personal satisfaction and self gratification. It will come as no surprise to learn that the strongest drive is for survival with 'self' at the head of the lifeboat queue. We all wear a large invisible neon sign which reads, 'Save me! Save me! Save me! Notice me! Notice me! Notice me!'

As the population explodes, society loses the personal touch; the individual merges into the human landscape and into a busy personal schedule. Little wonder then that we feel alone and need to be seen.

I heard a speaker quoting an author who said something like this and I apologise to the originator. I've been spreading it around as,

> 'Human existence is nothing more than a primal scream
> from the cradle to the grave in search of recognition'.

Pearce and the bottom line

Here is the bottom line again. As human beings we have one undying passion: Ourselves. Anyone who catches onto this will get our undying devotion. No matter how the gurus of the past and the boffins of the present dress it up, one fact is certain; the theme song of humanity is,

> A man I am, or woman
> A boy, a girl, a child
> I want to know you notice me
> The thought just drives me wild.

I can't offer you a reason
That anyone could see
Why I should get attention
But please just notice me.

I think, therefore I am
I've got a secret drive
My ego's running rampant
So please notice I'm alive.

You must understand that customers are your lifeblood but that they are complex, complicated, self-centred, selfish individuals. You cannot change that. You can only accept it and submit to it, pandering to them, caressing them and wooing them. It is not a pleasant sound or a pretty sight but it is true. You can't change it but don't worry, I will working on it for you behind the scenes.

Customers are your lifeblood but they are complex, complicated, self-centred, selfish individuals.

If you 'get it' and 'get it good' and operate out of this understanding you will live happily ever after. If you fight it, resent it, campaign or take up arms against it and STILL try to be in business you will be both miserable and broke.

FIVE STAR IDEA:
You will do best when you tattoo this behind your eyelids so it never leaves your sight:
Notice me. Talk about me. Focus on me. I am the nicest person in the world, the centre of the universe, the only person I think about from dawn till dusk. I am your customer.

LESSON 11

Reason #3 why you don't give five star service: You don't understand what business you are in

I started my life in sales working for a television station

I went out and talked people into buying some air time.

I knew nothing about sales. My one and only training session from the big boss was, 'Selling is like baseball, son. You can't hit 'em if you don't swing at 'em so there's the door, walk through and get out there swinging.'

That's what I did. I foot slogged the business district door to door, learning the craft of sales the hard way.

I'd no sooner have my foot through the door of a retail store than I'd hear a voice bark from behind the counter, 'What are you selling?' or 'Rep. day is Thursday thanks!'

In those early days when they asked me what I was selling I always answered, 'TV advertising'. I didn't know any better.

They weren't the easiest people in the world to talk to and it wasn't easy to explain in the half minute they normally gave me, but it didn't take me long to work out that I wasn't selling TV advertising at all.

I was there to keep their business in the main street. I was selling them more customers. I was selling them the prestige of appearing on TV and the credibility it gave them. I was selling them more money in the till. I was the hero on the white horse. Without me they would keep doing what they'd always been doing and would keep getting what they'd always got – mediocrity.

So what are you selling?

I meet people in seminars several times a week and when I ask them what they do for a living or what business they are in they have no idea. They think they do but they don't.

I ask travel agents, 'What business are you in?'

They say, 'Travel'.

The butcher says, 'I'm a butcher', the hot bread person says, 'I own a bakery', the women's fashion store owner says, 'I own a dress shop'.

Their employees are worse. They say, 'Shop assistant', or 'I just work in a dress shop'.

So what's wrong with that?

In one sense there's nothing wrong with it. It's definitive enough for a fast paced conversation. I do the same. On a plane when the person in the next seat asks me my occupation, I say, 'I speak at conferences'. It gets the playing surface clear. That's not the big deal.

What really gets to me is that's ALL they say. They don't know any better and that there is more they could say. It's the belief in what they do that's missing. It's knowing what business they are in so that it sticks out of them, lights up their eyes, shines their faces.

So what could they say?

There's a lot of fluff flying around from the try-hard eighties. Back in the days of the vision statement and the mission statement and the purpose driven corporation and the corporate ideal, everyone had to know what business they were in.

I contributed to the mythology by conducting seminars and writing video training packages about it.

People wasted hundreds of hours trying to nut out a pithy encapsulation of their purpose so they could hang it in a gold frame on the reception area wall.

I say they wasted their time because in the end after they had worn out the thesaurus and the dictionary, it generally didn't mean a bean to the team. They still didn't know why they came to work.

Ask the average printer why he came to work in the publishing house and he would say, 'To turn the machines on', or 'To get paid', or 'To print books'.

What are you doing?

This is a story that has been attributed to every famous architect and philosopher you can think of. I don't even know if it ever happened but it's a nice yarn. I attribute it to Sir Christopher Wren, who after the great fire of London in 1666 rebuilt 55 of the city's 87 churches including St Paul's Cathedral in 1710. It seems appropriate.

> In the midst of the extensive rebuilding programme after the great fire of London, Sir Christopher Wren often visited his building sites anonymously and chatted with the builders.
>
> One day he asked several carpenters one by one, what they were doing.
>
> The first muttered without looking up, 'Sawing a piece of wood'. Wren was disappointed with his answer and moved on.
>
> Another straightened his back a moment, surveyed his work and proudly said, 'I'm laying a floor'. Wren considered that the fellow had a much broader view of his work and complimented his workmanship.
>
> A third man stopped what he was doing and looking up to where the cathedral's spire would one day puncture the sky said, 'I'm helping the famous architect Sir Christopher Wren build a mighty cathedral of worship that will last for centuries to the glory of God'.

'I'm helping the famous architect Sir Christopher Wren build a mighty cathedral of worship that will last for centuries to the glory of God.'

Wren introduced himself and thanked the man for sharing his dream and for understanding his destiny in the overall scheme of history.

He 'got it' instinctively

The nice part about the story is that it illustrates how you don't need a mission statement if your heart is in the right place.

A mission statement is a very handy tool as we shall see but you ought to know instinctively what you are on about.

• You're not in the travel game. You help people have great and memorable holidays. You give them major milestones in their personal history. Once you understand this you find it easy and natural to recommend the best hotels and the finest tours and first class travel, as well as complimentary film processing with your colleagues in the film shop next door, and discount vouchers with the travelware retailer down the mall.

• You're not a butcher. You don't flog the flesh of dead animals. You are a facilitator of fine dining and happy family meal times and great social gatherings. More important things happen during the eating of the meals you help create than in all the parliaments of the world. Once you understand this you find it easy to pass out recipes, conduct cooking demonstrations, prepare pre-dressed meats and meal packs.

• You're not in the restaurant business. You don't cook stuff or make the best cappuccinos in town. You sell people the opportunity to talk business with their defences down. You make opportunities for lovers to rendezvous, for friends to bond and grow, for families to talk without the TV and the phone to distract them. Understanding this makes it easy for you to offer larger slices of cake, bigger serves of salad, nicer after-dinner chocolates and better hand towels in the washrooms.

• You're not a women's fashion retailer. You're not in the rag trade. You make women feel special, look pretty, have confidence, present themselves professionally, attract a mate, look good, appeal to their families, present a beautiful image, create a hit at a wedding or be the belle of the ball. This makes it easy for you to be patient while they choose, offer them a large choice of accessories and suggest other matching switch and swap garments.

FIVE STAR IDEA:
Don't worry about creating a mission statement for now. Freewheel your thoughts. Don't go past this point until you write on this page. This cannot be overlooked. Don't tell me you'll come back to it later. Do it now.

Write down a list of all the things you do for people.

Which of their needs do you meet?

How do you make their lives happier, easier, simpler, more exciting, less dangerous, more hopeful, less disrupted?

LESSON 12

Reason #4 why you don't give five star service: You understand what business you are in but you don't like doing it

Bummer!

You understand the business you are in but you just can't take it. It's no longer for you. You're just going through the motions. You open the store. You tend the counter. You take the money. You pack up the goods. You are courteous enough (except when you are pushed) but you just can't stand it any more.

There's no real purpose to your work – even your life.

And the worst news is you are the owner!

I know how that feels. So do countless others across the Western retail world. We expect to enjoy our work and decide whether it is meaningful enough for us before we'll agree to put our heart into it. It seems as though we have an epidemic of 'the right to enjoy our work'. Once upon a time people simply worked; down the mine, at the forge, at the mill, in the paddock and the helm. They didn't think about anything but death separating them from their lot in life.

We're getting choosier

As you've noticed, that's all changed.

Most of us are well enough educated and multi-skilled to pick and choose between many options in a lifetime. Whether that is right or wrong is not for me to judge. It is however the reality of today's working environment.

So little wonder that you might be reading these lessons wondering whether you'll ever be able to develop a passion for what you do.

Take the test

Here's a few simple questions to clear your head:

1 a) Are you really at your wits' end or
b) Do you just need a holiday?

If a) go to question 2.

If b) go on a holiday and come back a nicer person or if your holidays are not due, get longer sleep, exercise a bit more, eat less fat and sugar and don't rage so much on your days off. You might be surprised at how much better your job looks after a week of early nights. You'll certainly look better.

2 a) Is the job you are in the only one you can get or
b) Are your skills instantly portable?

If a) either

(i) stay where you are and get to like it or

(ii) start a study course that will equip you with new skills for either a promotion or a new job, or

(iii) compound your problems ten-fold by leaving and not having a job,

but please don't stay there wasting space.

If b) give fair notice and go find somewhere else to work so you can catch on fire with a new purpose.

3 a) Do you just think a change will do you good?
b) Do you understand that every job requires you to have passion about it?

If a) remember that shifting a dead body to a new coffin will not bring it back to life. You'll simply be taking your worms with you. You need to sort out why you're on the planet first.

If b) as in 2 b) above, give fair notice and go find somewhere else to work so you can catch on fire with a new purpose.

4 a) Can you see your job as a training experience for something greater or
b) Is it as if you are in gaol, at a dead end, cut off at the pass?

If a) settle in and learn as much as you can, about the product, the business, management and customers. A well worked job is like a well ploughed field, sown for a plentiful harvest.

> I was with Peter Elligett, a client who had grown up in the McDonald's Family Restaurant business and had become an area manager before joining another firm.
>
> We were chatting about a current affairs television programme I'd seen where members of a studio audience were explaining why they had the right to refuse work if they found the work below their dignity. One young man had been featured saying, 'I just think my life has more purpose than standing behind a counter all day asking, "Would you like fries with that?"' The audience had applauded wildly in mutual appreciation of his derisive comment.
>
> Peter related how the night before he had attended an anniversary celebration at the first McDonald's Restaurant opened in Australia where the guests included many former employees. The guests had also commented on the television programme.
>
> It was a source of great hilarity for them as they checked the guest list, counting the number of surgeons, dentists, lawyers, accountants, millionaires, entrepreneurs and philanthropists in the room who had all started their working life asking, 'Would you like fries with that?'

If b) then make way for your gift. If you have another passion and it will do the world a great good to let it free then you had better make a fast track toward it and get on with it. You only have one go at life and you've already wasted a great lump of it. If you're the owner of the store go see the landlord and beg to be released. The landlord would rather have a live business in your location than a dead one.

5 a) Do you know what you want to do or
b) Are you still working it out?

If a) then go do it. If it will pay you a cheque in the first week as big or bigger than the one you're getting now, then nothing should hold you back. Do look before you leap.

If b) write out an ideal picture of what you would rather do for people and determine if anyone will pay you for it. If they will pay you then make haste. Let not the world be without your contribution a moment longer. My fifteen-year old twins and about forty of their friends want to be rock stars rather than join the job scene. Because they are young and silly they can't see the sense of my question, 'But what will you eat when the only people who like that horrible racket you make are other rock bands who also haven't got any money to pay to hear you?'

FIVE STAR IDEA:
Make up your mind now. Start over in something new and meaningful or grind it out where you are. Just do it. Suck it up and get the job done with dignity. There are few things more dignifying to the human spirit than purposeful, disciplined, rewarding work.

LESSON 13

REASON #5 WHY YOU DON'T GIVE FIVE STAR SERVICE: YOU HAVEN'T WORKED OUT YOUR POLICIES, PROCEDURES AND PROMISES

Tough work if you can handle it

This chapter should be a book in its own right but no-one would read it. It's like sleeping in a tent on stony ground. You can handle it for two nights because of the adventure but by the third day you pack up for home.

You need someone like me to tackle you on all these issues. I can't see many readers attending to all of them though. If you complete a few of these exercises you will still be a mile in front. If you want to be a real achiever, address them all.

Two dozen searching questions

Whether you're in a strong or struggling position, answering these questions will help clear your sinuses. It will show you where you stand in the broad scope. You can't tell the health of a business just by looking at its balance sheet. That only tells you about its money.

He has clogged arteries, massive cholesterol, arthritis, diabetes, and ingrown toenails. And that's not all! He's also dead!

Naturally, if the business doesn't have enough money to survive, this exercise is like doing a health check on a corpse.

1. Are we secure financially?
2. Are we profitable?
3. Do we have a stable and dedicated staff?
4. Are we doing what we are supposed to be doing – ie baking bread, fitting tyres?
5. Are we doing what our board or owners or shareholders or franchisors want us to do?

But in thinking deeper

6. Are we as financially secure as we *could* be?
7. Are we as profitable as we *might* be?
8. Is having *stable and dedicated* staff the most we should be expecting as an employer, and are we *challenging* each other?
9. Are we stretching ourselves to serve as many people as we can?
10. Are we doing *more* than what our board or owners or shareholders or franchisors want us to do?

Apart from that, in order to fulfil our mission ...

11. Are we as fully aware of the extent and capacity of our market as we ought to be?
12. Are we as innovative as we could be?
13. Have we assiduously thought through the implications of technology on our position in ten years' time? For example, will there be a need for our product or service as we know the process now? If so how might they be produced? If not, what might we offer in place of them?

I asked these questions of a book printer in 1993 and the film and plate makers said, 'They'll always need good old-fashioned trades like ours'. Tomorrow the company will install a press which takes computer art to finished product just like a big sophisticated ink jet printer, by-passing several of those 'old-fashioned' trades.

In 1994, the Internet had so few web sites, Jerry Yang, co-founder of the big search engine Yahoo would have been able to find them all in an afternoon. As I write, Yahoo now records over 31 million unique visitors a month and yet it only boasts of searching a third of the available sites. In late 1997 the competitive effect of the Internet was so intense that Encyclopedia Brittanica cancelled the contracts of all of its field sales staff. People asked, why buy a $1500 set of books when you can look up stuff on the internet for $20 a month?

14 Is our level of excellence so attractive that people come to us to find out how we are doing it so well?

15. Are we leaving no stone unturned in finding ways to be the best we can be?

16. Do we train our people to a level of excellence no competitor can match?

17. Do we know the real strengths of all our people?

18. Do we tap into the creative resources of our staff?

19. Do our people believe that they have a contributing interest in the destiny of our firm?

20. Are we opening up new markets?

21. Are we noted without fail for our quality of product and service?

22. Do we have increasing numbers of 'customers' beating a path to our door imploring us to sell to them?

23. If someone came to us with an assignment we would not normally take on, but with stretching we could complete, is there a structure by which we could draw on the divergent resources of our people and accept the assignment anyway?

24. In our staff is there that attractive Disney-like quality that keeps them looking and behaving in a dynamic and impeccable manner?

These questions encompass quite challenging expectations. They are questions a healthy organisation should ask itself periodically. They are questions you could invite each member of staff to ask of herself or himself. If you have too many 'No' answers or you find the questions frustrating it could be because you have missed developing some of the system stuff.

System stuff

Do you have a written corporate philosophy including

- ❑ Your mission statement
- ❑ Your values
- ❑ Your guiding principles and duty statements
- ❑ Your beliefs and intentions
- ❑ Your service promise
- ❑ Your business plan
- ❑ Your marketing plan
- ❑ Your goals

It suddenly got quiet around here.

Five objectives

Your objectives in undertaking this project are:

1. To capture and state those good driving forces which exist but which as yet are unrecorded.

2. To help your employees see and understand why you are in business and to allow everyone to measure their commitment to it.

3. To so place the mission before your people that they will re-commit to it.

4. To provide an instrument by which you can capture valuable insights and suggestions from your people.

5. To allow each person or department the opportunity to fine-tune individual objectives.

How long will this take?

I doubt if this can be done in the first reading. It might take a day. It might take a month of evenings with the TV turned off.

Four things you will get

1. An open statement of your Mission: Why you are here.

2. A strong concept of exactly what your organisation or department plans to achieve: What you are going to do.

3. An opportunity for everyone to 'own' the goals of the organisation and for every person to understand the big picture: Where everyone fits in.

4. A clear understanding of the way you want to manage your resources: Your people, your facilities, your client base and your finances: How you intend to do things.

It's a foundation

Once you've done it you can

• Take the initiative in your business and your market sector; to take the ball on the front foot as it were; to be pro-active rather than re-active.

• Experience better teamwork, coordination between staff or across departments.

• Draw on the experience and skill of all your staff.

Save lots of money

If you paid big time consultants thousands of dollars they still wouldn't think of all of these issues. Many consultants haven't done it for themselves! You don't have to pay me to do it for you because I'm already telling you what to do for just the cost of this book. Lucky you. So do it.

FIVE STAR IDEA:
Take the time to complete the next seven lessons. Don't be fooled by some of the brief introductions. The lesson is still important.

LESSON 14

Reason #6 why you don't give five star service: There's something wrong with your mission statement

Four possibilities here:

1. You have a mission statement and everyone of your team knows it, understands it and lives by it. Huge! That's what it's for.
2. You don't understand the importance of having a mission statement.
3. You *do* understand the importance of having a mission statement but you haven't bothered to do anything about it.
4. The mission statement you have written is wrong.

What is a mission statement?

Pay attention now because most mission statements you see are rubbish.

A mission statement is the hook you hang your business's hat on. It's what gets you up in the mornings when the floor is cold and the bed is warm. It is the inspirational, guiding statement about our purpose and direction. You already addressed this in part in Lesson 9.

It tells you where you're headed, what you're 'on about' and what drives the company forward. This is the heart of why you exist. It is your charter. Everything you do is gauged by it. You recruit new employees by it. You measure your performance by it and you use it to discipline yourself.

Joe Flower writing about Disney in *Prince of the Magic Kingdom* (John Wiley and Sons, Inc., New York, 1991, pp 262) writes

> Money alone is not enough to drive a company. A company has to be about something. Maytag is about reliability. American Express is about service. K-Mart is about low prices. When today's adults were growing up, Disney was not about something as simple as reliability or conservative accounting procedures. It was not, as some Disney people say today's Disney is, about 'quality'. It was not even about 'family entertainment'. It was about all that makes life precious: a sense of wonder, of adventure, of striving for greatness, of the genius of creativity. Its tone was moral and its product was myth and magic. Disney was about how to live.

Activity: You'll get a hold of your mission by answering whichever of these questions you find clearest and then summarising what you find into one comprehensive statement:
What are you on about?
Where are you going?
Why are you here?
What is your purpose in existing?

Sam Walton, founder of Walmart knew his mission. (*Sam Walton Made in America, My Story* Doubleday, New York, 1992, pp 51)

> The idea was simple: when customers thought of Wal-Mart, they should think of low prices and satisfaction guaranteed. They could be pretty sure they wouldn't find it cheaper anywhere else, and if they didn't like it, they could bring it back.

How long should it be?

Don't let some know-all tell you it isn't good enough if you can't say it in fifteen words. At the same time if you can't put it down in less than fifty you might not be all that clear. Start by writing it out in as many words as you feel it needs and then prune it down to a hundred and then fifty and then maybe twenty-five if you like.

You're not writing an advertising slogan or a logo caption. It doesn't have to be slick or cute. You're not trying to impress the people at the club. You're defining why you're in business.

Some things it doesn't have to be but it can be if you like.

It doesn't have to be framed.

It doesn't have to be stamped in bronze on the wall.

It doesn't have to be in Latin.

Mine is. It is

Si amigos dere dego. Forte loris innaro.

De ant loris. De is trux fullov orsis cousan dux.#

#Turn page upside down for translation

See amigos. There they go. Forty lorries in a row.

They ain't lorries, they is trucks, full of horses, cows and ducks.

LESSON 15

Reason #7 why you don't give five star service: You're not in touch with your values

Clarifying your values helps you state what you prize most about what you do and the people for whom you perform your service.

An egg farmer for example, might believe that packing brown eggs with white eggs together gives customers a feeling of 'farm goodness'. He would expect all his employees to pack egg cartons with both brown and white eggs, because he values the feeling his pack gives the consumer.

There might be an employee of the egg farmer who values *freshness* and wants to introduce the practice of leaving a downy feather in each carton to give customers a feeling of 'farm goodness *AND freshness!*' The two value systems need to be discussed and the final decision made about whether the feather is important or whether it is rather a red herring.

Understanding your core values will give you direction. Values are about what you do.

Activity: Write up a sentence or two about your values as they impact each of these: (Think about it now. No motherhood statements or slogans)

What do I think about people?

____

____

How do I feel about customers?

____

____

What is my view of my team members? (If you think of them as 'staff' then that's a value right there)

____

____

What is my approach to the topic of work?

____

____

How do I feel about cooperation?

____

____

How do I rate my attitude to competitiveness?

What do I think about free enterprise?

What priority do I give service?

What is my approach to equal opportunity?

How do I define communication?

I'm sure there are other values you hold which impact your business. Make some notes about those too.

LESSON 16

REASON #8 WHY YOU DON'T GIVE FIVE STAR SERVICE: YOU'RE BLURRY ON YOUR GUIDING PRINCIPLES OR DUTY STATEMENTS

The egg farmer I mentioned before would need to specify an exact number of brown eggs to include in each pack, otherwise his employees will not accurately reflect his values and his image might change. His packers could also become confused and less productive.

Every organisation has rules which direct the way you interact with your team and your customers and the way you do your work. Sometimes the rules are spoken and sometimes they are unspoken. They need to be captured and written down so everyone knows what to do.

Even organisations that say they have no rules have the rule that says there are no rules.

From the start

Before they start on the job, (even before the initial interview), new employees need to read the mission statement, the values and the duty statements and you need to ask whether the new people have the wherewithal to comply.

If they don't, please don't hire them.

Guiding Principles are about *how* you do things, and you'll typically find these items in a procedures manual, but someone (you) has to disassemble them and affix them to individuals' instruction sheets for them to be of any use.

> I was at a conference of a significant franchise company and we asked the one hundred and seventy people present how many had referred to the company's manuals in the last three months. One new person had. No-one else had referred to the manuals in either the last six months or the previous twelve. Four had never opened them at all. The chairman pointed out that even if those stores had been functioning at peak performance, they would make their job so much easier if they would interpret the manuals to their teams.

And by way of fair warning, it's no use working out your 'hows' before you work out your 'whats' and 'whys'. You need to go back to the previous lessons if you skipped them.

Don't opt for the Weekend at Bernie's approach

> It's a great movie. Two young guys get to use a rich person's house for the weekend only to find that the owner (Bernie) has died and in order to protect themselves from being accused of murder they have to make it look like he is alive. They take poor old dead Bernie everywhere, up stairs, down stairs, to parties, even skiing and once drop him off a balcony. To all appearances he looks alive – but he's as dead as Nero.

Sometimes business owners call on me to 'fix' their business. They want me to train their staff or install some new behaviours to give the place a lift but I often have to say, 'The impossible I can normally handle but this business needs a chocolate coated pill from Miracle Max'. You can't prop up a business with systems when the heart has stopped. No how-to's will stick where a business has a terminal illness.

Why can't I fix them?

They either didn't do the work in this lesson before they started or they bought a business from someone else who hadn't done it and they're stuck with the wrong people and no culture of success and service. They have to go right back to the start with everyone and get the culture right. All they can expect is pain until they get it right.

I've seen others who designed their service systems to suit themselves and to make their life easier. That's why they put up signs that antagonise and niggle customers.

No cheques

Minimum purchase on credit strictly $10

No refunds

No returns without a receipt

Don't touch

You break it. You pay for it

You want it when?

Don't sit on the furniture

Don't handle the merchandise

Look but don't touch

Keep your hands off the glass

Strictly no admittance. Staff only

Use other door

Wrong door

Deliveries in side street

Shut the !!^%**$£@ door!

Parking space reserved for manager

I loved the sign in the loading bay of a steel tubing store. They said what they wanted to say without giving offence. They wanted customers to keep out of the way while they were cutting steel. The sign said,

If we cut it, it's free
If you cut it, it's $5 a cut
If you help us cut it, it's $10 a cut.

By that sign the management had reinforced their value systems about safety for the team, respect for the customers, and their guiding principle had come over in good humour.

Think about how the customer would prefer to do business with you so you see it from outside the store, not from your side of the counter.

Activity: Write out a few comments about each of the following

How do you rate quality?

____

____

What is value for money?

____

____

What is continuous improvement?

____

____

Why is accuracy important?

____

____

What part does punctuality play?

What attitude do you want your team to have to your suppliers?

On what basis would you allow your team to discount your prices? (If at all)

Your guiding principles should turn into systems and practices like

How should the day start?

How should a shift change?

How should the store close?

How is the money handled, checked and banked?

How are returns managed?

Who is called on when there is sickness?

How are robberies handled?

What do you do about shoplifting?

What do you do about complaints?

What do you do about refunds?

FIVE STAR IDEA:
Take this seriously. This is just the beginning. Every time you establish policy, write it down. When you find a discrepancy in procedures because people are working out of different values or interpretations, make policy and write it in your Guiding Principles book. If it's not written down and tattooed on the backs of their eyelids it's Rafferty's Rules out there.

LESSON 17

Reason #9 why you don't give five star service: You're not in touch with your beliefs and intentions

Values guide what you do. Beliefs help you understand why you do them.

There are distinctive beliefs in your corporate structure which are rooted in your history and tradition and these have cast you in a mould distinctly your own. You're not like everyone else. Neither is your business. Even if you belong to a franchise group I know from years of hard won experience that there are no two the same. This is because of the beliefs of the operators.

This exercise will help you to lay your beliefs on the table and you may even be able to question the validity of some of them.

> I'm sure you know the story of the young husband who asked his wife why she cut the last six inches off the leg of lamb before she cooked it.
> 'That's the way you cook lamb. Everyone knows that', she told him as if he was silly.
> 'My mother didn't do it that way', he said.

'Well she doesn't know how to cook lamb then! Ask my mother and ask Grandma. It's how you bring out the taste', she retorted. Not wanting to make a scene he kept his peace.

When his mother-in-law came to visit he asked her if she also cut the last six inches off the leg of lamb. 'Of course dear', she replied. 'It's been passed down through the family for years. Ask Grandma. She'll tell you. It brings out the juices.' He couldn't wait to find out why his own mother had been so ignorant of this important culinary fact, so he was most anxious to ask the old grandmother all about it. He called on her to ask.

'Grandmother, why do you cut the last six inches off the leg of lamb?'

Looking down her nose at him, as if he had no brains at all, she said, 'Otherwise it would be too long to fit in my little oven'.

Eager to let his bride and mother-in-law into the secret he scurried home to tell them but together they chorused, 'It doesn't matter why she does it. It still tastes better this way.'

Mother and daughter had taken a small occurrence and built several myths around it until the myths had become bigger than the truth.

Your business could be full of myths. You might have someone on your team who habitually treats men with contempt or who gives women discounts or who charges rich people more or who regards anyone with an accent as 'an ethnic' and therefore needing to be treated with suspicion.

Here are three examples of such myths and their fruits.

You've got an accent so that proves you're stupid.

I didn't know what it was like to be treated as a second class citizen until I lived in the USA. Still one of my favourite places and full of some of my favourite people I noticed nevertheless that having an accent put me on the outer edge of social acceptance.

> I'd never thought of myself as having an accent (or for that matter being foreign) until after speaking at a teachers' convention one day in Florida, one of the teachers asked my wife to pass on his compliments to me for my excellent command of English and then asked what language we spoke in our native land of Australia.
>
> It became clearer when I called companies on the phone.
>
> I'd ask for Mr Brown and the receptionist would ask my name.
>
> 'Colin Pearce', I'd say.
>
> She'd say, 'Pardon me?'
>
> 'Colin Pearce.'
>
> 'Pardon me?'
>
> 'Colin Pearce.'
>
> 'Pardon me?'
>
> Fed up, I'd give in and assume the accent, 'Kah-lun PiRRRss'.
>
> Not satisfied with that she'd then typically go through the routine of
>
> 'Where are you from?'
>
> 'No company. Just me myself.'
>
> 'Pardon me?'

> And so around it would go again.
>
> After a few days of this I simply decided to invent a company and say, 'I'm from Oppenweid, Leenbach, and Belch!'
>
> (Say it over aloud a couple of times and you'll get wind of what I was up to.)
>
> It seemed to satisfy them and I still had the last laugh.

If your skin is a different colour, you can't count.

You might have people in your business who unwittingly let customers know they don't belong. You might have started it yourself because of your own beliefs. I met a manager who was horrified that one of his team members had sworn at an Aboriginal man for wanting to pay for a small item with a large denomination note. I told him I wasn't surprised, because he himself had given the lad permission to reject the customer by starring at the weekly Friday night drinks hour with tasteless jokes about Aboriginals.

Beware of Greeks

I consulted for another company who had a standing joke that the company would not accept orders from Greeks.

> At their Christmas parties one of the partners always regaled the gathering with the story of their beginnings when they, in their naivete, had allowed themselves to be swindled by a customer. The customer just happened to have a Greek name, and the partner telling the story would begin it by saying, 'Then one day this Greek bloke came along with short arms and deep pockets...' and he'd finish it with '... and that's why from that day to this we don't accept orders from Greeks'.

Some of the sales team over the years had become so convinced that the statement reflected the owners' beliefs that they would deliberately not offer their product to Greek people, and they made especially sure by also not offering the products to anyone they thought might be Greek just by their appearance, which included Italians, Lebanese, Spaniards, Maltese, Iranians – you name it.

When I revealed this to the owners they were incredulous. They had unwittingly isolated themselves from several lucrative market niches.

Is it possible that you are unwittingly alienating people because of your beliefs?

Is it also possible that you are fully aware of your beliefs but can see now that you are robbing yourself because of them?

Activity: Define what you believe about ...

Customers in your area.

Are there some that you believe need watching for dishonesty, or who try to cheat you out of your price by haggling. Is this based on a scientific fact or just on some old duffer's tale you read on a fringe political party's pamphlet. Remember these might be the people who feed your family.

____

____

____

What do you believe about landlords, or franchisors or head office people? Again is this based on fact or prejudice or sound judgement?

And if your beliefs are based on sound judgement are they doing you any good?

Do you have set thinking patterns on change?

How about honesty – declaring all your cash income as taxable, removing stock for gifts or to take home without noting it in the cash drawer? The team member pilfering from you might simply be mirroring your own beliefs?

Really now, what do you believe about customers?

LESSON 18

Reason #10 why you don't give five star service: You haven't defined your service promise

Service promises were big in the eighties, but they were treated like a fad and went the way of the dinosaurs. They shouldn't have. They were just what we needed and we're crying out for them today.

A service promise defines what everyone can expect; employees and customers alike. Companies included their service promises in advertising, on wall plaques and in brochures.

> At Macca's you knew they'd deliver your order in a minute. You wouldn't be left in a queue with more than four people in it before someone opened a new service line. At Shell service stations they'd fix your car or it was free. At Pizza Hut your lunch time pizza was delivered in ten minutes or it was on the house. At the banks you were attended to within five minutes or you got five dollars in your account. At Budget your phone call was answered within five rings or you got five dollars off your first day's rental.

Part of the reason that service promises didn't catch on more widely was that they were a bit over the top. The least practical examples were written by swank management consultants and dumped on the staff at big corporate dinners. Naturally enough the staff didn't buy in.

Others were worked out by teams of excited young hopefuls at a retreat who couldn't live up to their own expectations when they got back to work.

What's it for?

A service promise lays out what customers can expect and lets every team member know how to meet those expectations.

> Remember the Comet freight commercials on TV? 'If this package isn't in Adelaide by tomorrow, it's Y.O.U.R. job.' You saw everyone at the various levels of responsibility at Comet passing the package along the line sounding the warning to the next person in the pecking order.

It has to be consistent

Be careful about letting some employees develop their own service promise. 'I like to do this for my customers', they say. On the surface of it you'd think this should be worthy of reward. However when their customers meet another team member who has no knowledge of the first team member's service promise, those customers become confused and disappointed with the organisation. You can't have rogue 'do-gooders'.

Activity: Define what you really want to do for every customer and ask this question: Can we do it? If it's do-able one hundred percent of the time, then make it a promise. Here's a guide.

Promises you can't keep even though you'd like to

(These would be better as team guidelines only because they are too hard to perform every time.)

We'll smile at every customer

We'll make eye contact with every customer

We'll attend to every customer within thirty seconds of their approaching the counter

We'll have your product in stock

We'll get out-of-stock product in twenty-four hours

Our prices are the lowest in town

Our service is the friendliest in town

In fact anything with 'est' in it is impossible to uphold.

Promises you can keep

Every item will be gift wrapped

If we can't answer your question about a product we'll call the supplier for you

We give 5% discount for cash

If it's not in stock and we've advertised it, we'll deliver it free when it's available

We will not keep you on hold on the phone for longer than... seconds

Unhappy with something? Bring it back and we will give you a full cash refund.

So here's a space to start your list of promises:

FIVE STAR IDEA:
Before you publish your service promise, share it with some loyal customers and see if they think it is what they'd expect from you? If you're off the track, no matter how good it sounds, burn it and start again.

LESSON 19

Reason #11 why you don't give five star service: You don't even know what you do best so you wobble all over the market place

What you do best is called your 'Sustainable Competitive Advantage'

You are unique as an organisation. There are some characteristics about you and some aspects of your organisation which give you a distinct advantage over your competition. They translate into your Unique Selling Propositions which we'll look at next.

I help companies work through this complete corporate philosophy because sometimes they find it hard to recognise their best strengths. Here's a sample list we worked up for the people who printed this book, Open Book Publishers.

- Complete In-House editorial, design, production and distribution capability
- Functioning wholesale distribution
- Profitable, established retail stores throughout the country
- Highly efficient operation and service
- Stable ownership, management, and staff
- Strong capitalised finance backing
- General Manager and Editor appointed by the board

guaranteeing their willingness to work in concurrence with the board's mission statement
- Consistent succession plan in place from one generation of managers to the next
- Proven track record in publishing for Australia and for export

As a publisher myself I choose the printing arm of Open Book because the company has sustained these competitive advantages over seventy years and they offer me sound advice and reliability. Neither the cheapest nor the most flamboyant they offer quality, dependability and friendship. And they do that consistently for every customer.

Knowing this has enabled them to stay focused on their core business. They thought about installing a quick book system, where customers bring in their disk and a machine turns the whole thing into a book in a flash. But they decided that they should continue to work with their strengths as design and layout experts and build their reputation as a best-result-for-you printer.

This is something they know they can sustain. It's not something that is here today and passed over tomorrow. That's what makes Open Book competitive. They resisted the urge to follow the crowd with discounting and now as printers all around them are falling over for lack of cash flow, they are mopping up. That's what being competitive means: They are still in the competition.

Activity: Write down what makes you strong; not necessarily different or better. It's what you can sustain over a long time and is probably the core of what you do.

- Do you bake cookies in a quick bake machine? That's yours. You wouldn't want to meander off into jelly babies.

- Do you have a strong franchisor who is behind you all the way? That's yours. You wouldn't want to wander off and become independent.

- Is your landlord providing shoppers with a safe, clean environment with accessible parking? Latest surveys show that's what they want. If so, then that's one of your sustainable competitive advantages.

My sustainable competitive advantage is: ______________________

____

____

____

____

____

LESSON 20

Reason #11 why you don't give five star service: You can't put your finger on your USPs

Your USPs are your Unique Selling Propositions.

There are some things you can do that no-one else does. Isolating and understanding these will help you to position yourself properly in your market, and contend for business better than your competitors can. You'll be able to offer your customers exactly what you're good at instead of offering them a fist full of everything.

It works the same for me.

I'm a speaker. I am really good at these topics: Add-on selling, customer service, telephone sales and team relationships. I'm also an engaging storyteller. I'm not boasting any more than you are when you tell me you make great coffee or sell highest quality suits. It's a fact. Given time to prepare I can speak on anything else; I'll still make you laugh and provoke you to good deeds but you get the best value from me when you get me to speak or consult with you on my strong topics.

Here's the list of USPs we worked out for Open Book, springing from their Sustainable Competitive Advantages.

- We are the leading printer of genealogy and family history, so we can manage customer's projects capably.
- We are experienced in all aspects of editorial and publishing, so we can handle manuscripts and projects generated either by us or by customers.
- Although we have expertise as a general printer we are more experienced as book publishers and magazine printers.
- Having stable staff means that a customer is likely to work with the same person or team of people the next time he comes to do business with us.
- The capabilities of our Trade and Distribution department mean that we are able to distribute products to the widest possible markets in Australia.
- We are skilled and experienced hymn book publishers and printers and best positioned to serve that kind of clientele.

Activity: Translate your competitive advantages into unique selling propositions. Think of what makes your customer's eyes sparkle. Think about aspects of your business that make you excited when you deliver them. They are probably your unique selling propositions. This is a toughie. Maybe you should take a break and come back to it when you are full of fight again.

____

____

____

____

LESSON 21

Reason #13 why you don't give five star service: You don't know what you want your customers to say after you've served them

Are you supposed to know what you want your customers to say after you've served them?

You may well respond,

> 'I want them to say, "Goodbye".'
> 'What's wrong with them saying, "See ya later"?'
> 'I hope mine say they are leaving the neighbourhood.'
> 'Why do they have to say anything?'

At first glance you might think this could not possibly be important. Why do you have to know what your customers will say after you've served them?

It's a test
Simple. When they say it you'll know you did what you intend to do, and when they don't say it you'll know you're slipping.
It is possible to write down the kind of comments you hope to receive from your customers. These are the remarks you hope they

would make after experiencing your service while purchasing your products. It is a way of helping you commit to the quality of workmanship to which you say you aspire. We call them 'ideal customer comments'.

They shape your behaviour
Set down the comments you want to hear and you'll find that you begin to manipulate your interactions in order to elicit the responses you long for. Slowly but surely you'll fashion your behaviour into a new shape which finally demands the desired response.

You might be happy with hearing them say, 'Thank you'.

Here is a list to which other businesses have contributed:

> I want them to say 'Wow!'
> I want them to look me in the eye and say 'Thank you' and really mean it.
> I want them to go out laughing for joy at the experience.
> I want my customers to ask if they can bring back a friend.
> I want customers to tell me they will be back.
> I want customers to ask me to tell them when our new range comes in.
> I want customers to ask if they can go on a mailing list for brochures.
> I want customers to tell me they have never had such a good meal.
> I want to take their breath away so they can't say anything.
> I want their eyes to fill with tears of surprise.

I want them to smile all the way home.

I want them to come in saying they heard about us from the hot gossip down at the bridge club.

Activity: Write out your list of ideal customer statements.

____

____

____

____

FIVE STAR IDEA:
Discuss anything that is standing in the way of getting to the place where you hear those ideal statements every time and what you are going to do to remove the blockage.

3

SECTION

Why you SHOULD give five star service on a one star budget

Near enough is not good enough. It is no longer enough for you and your four neighbouring shops in your quarter-mile radius to open the doors at 9:00 am and close it at 5:00 pm and expect to make a living. Some folks pine for those days when life was that simple, but they are long gone – along with iron cars, the Hula Hoop, 12" LP records, Box Brownie cameras, Annette Funicello and the Mouseketeers.

You can't make it without pizzazz, panache and a penchant for parades and parties. You have to like your customers and entertain them or they will simply take their wallets and purses to one of the two hundred and forty shops next door.

LESSON 22

WHY DO SOME STORES LOSE CUSTOMERS AND COULD IT HAPPEN TO YOU?

Question: Why do some stores lose customers?

Good question.

The answer: Because they keep employing silly people.

May I make a phone call?

> A friend, David, went to town to buy a gift for the retiring president of an association of which he is the treasurer.
>
> 'A little bird' in the retiring president's office had leaked it out that she had long held a secret ambition to own a quality tortoiseshell fountain pen.
>
> David went into a big store and asked to see the tortoiseshell pens. Like me he thought tortoises only came in one colour so when he was confronted by a choice of three colours he knew he could make a terrible mistake if he chose the wrong one. He knew he had to ring the informant.
>
> So he asked, *'Can I use a phone?'*
>
> The assistant said, *'Yes. There's one upstairs by the elevators.'*
>
> A little annoyed that he wasn't offered the one on the counter he trotted upstairs, to find – you guessed it – a pay phone. On trying to use it he found it was out of order.

> Then he toddled out into the mall to find a public phone. You're wondering if I'm making this up. I'm not.
> He found the phone and checked the colour for the pen, but while he was on the phone he noticed he was standing outside a gift shop. When he inquired if they stocked pens he discovered they kept the very same as the big store. Same price. Same colour. So he bought the gift there.

And to think the big store had him right there in their clutches and they let his $170 sale get away just over the price of a local 23 cent phone call.

Yes they hire silly people. And who's the silliest? The management team!
Why?

Aloof rule makers

They've worked on the golden rule:

They who have the gold make the rules.

Without walking the shop floor or thinking through how their rule will be interpreted they've issued an edict. I can see it clearly. Management sent out a memo which read,

'Counter phones are not to be used for private calls'.

But they didn't spell out to the staff in words of one syllable or less, the very essence of loving, supportive, pro-active selling skills.

Do what you can to solve the customer's problem then and there on the spot – whatever it is. A customer walking away is likely to buy from someone else, or buy something inferior.

The sales assistant needed to say, 'Yes. I'll get a line for you and you can call from here. Is that alright?' but she couldn't because she feared the repercussions of breaking the rules.

I can see a finance person even now reading these lines and exclaiming, 'But if we let every customer use the phone, think what the phone bill would be!'

I guess it might be higher than it is now, but that's not the point is it? The point is that worrying about telephone use is just a symptom of a much larger problem: Aloof rule makers dominating the customer service culture and consequently creating rule-bound staff.

Just swap it over

> Another man told me how a rule-bound salesperson had nearly led him to committing murder. He'd bought a hose fitting for his washing machine at a manufacturer's spare parts counter.
> Unaware that the fittings came in two sizes he'd neglected to check the size of his fittings. Confronted by this revelation at the counter he was offered the option of taking the fitting of his choice and on the chance that it was the wrong one he could bring it back. 'You've got a 50:50 chance of being right', said the cheery salesperson. 'Take a chance.'
> On arriving home he could see straight away that the fitting was the wrong size so he threw it back in the car unopened, to return the next day.

A little annoyed with himself but in reasonably good spirits because of the pleasant interactions of the day before he called on the spare parts place and plonked the fitting on the counter with a sheepish grin. 'Wrong one hey? Don't buy a lottery ticket today then!' said the cheerful fellow.

'Yes, I need the small one. Can't win can you?'

'Got your receipt?'

Later when he thought about it, no matter how he replayed that scene over in his mind and no matter what he suggested to himself about what could have been said, there was never going to be a satisfactory response to that question.

'No, sorry', he said patting his pockets in mock embarrassment. 'I left it in my other coat.'

'Can't help you then. Need a receipt.'

Panic set in. he could sense that this was not going to be a good experience.

'But it's me. I was here yesterday. You know me. I'm the 50:50 guy.'

'I know who you are but it doesn't change the fact that I need a receipt.'

The salesperson had stopped being cheery and had assumed an officious and nasty tone. The customer started to heat up too.

'How about we use our common sense here? The two items are the same price. There's no difference but the size and the peg they hang on. Just reach over and grab the other one and while you're there, put this one back, and I'll be out of your hair.'

'Read the sign mate! No exchanges without proof of purchase. Give us your receipt and you can have it. Either that or buy the one you want. Otherwise I'm not going to argue about it.'

'Look...' sputtered the customer but he was interrupted.

'No you look. We get this all the time and then we get it in the neck from management about our stock adjustments, and it's people like you that make our life impossible. No exchange without a receipt. That's it.'

The customer told me he wanted to leap across the counter and choke the salesperson to death. He hates the company, hates his washing machine, will never buy that brand again and has told his story to hundreds of people.

'Win the argument and lose the customer' seemed to be the rule.

Hrmph and Ermf

And you know how that ridiculous scenario came about don't you? In a board meeting far far away in another galaxy an accountant looked at the stock figures and found a few discrepancies. The sales director pointed out that the discrepancies were caused by 'the lads' at the counters using their discretion and commonsense and that a few losses were inevitable. The accountant hrmphed and ermfed and after his neck blew a bubble he moved a motion that no returns be issued without receipts and it was carried with only one dissenting vote and became law. It was passed down the line as such without any riders or 'give' and so the company lost more through that practice than they had been losing through the other. But at least the accountant had all the receipts. Daft!

Activity: Part one – Make a list of suggestions about how the department store and the washing machine company could have handled the customer 'situations'.

___

___

___

___

___

Part two - Examine your rules and see if some are open to misinterpretations by unsuspecting loyal team members. If so, reinterpret or change them.

___

___

___

___

___

- There ought to be a margin for the 'use your brain' factor.
- There ought to be a reward for the best incident about keeping the customer happy while costing the company the least.
- There ought to be recognition for speed of recovery.
- There ought to be a reward for the best rule-breaking story which earned the most respect or the most business for the company.

FIVE STAR IDEA:
Make it easy to do business with you.

LESSON 23

SOMEONE RAISED THE BAR

I was eleven years old. It was summer 1959. My father had died and my mother was taking me on a bus holiday to Queensland. We broke the journey by staying over one night at an hotel in Sydney. To stretch our legs after two days on the bus we strolled out in the street before bedtime and that night I was baptised into the latter half of the twentieth century.

Mum and I experienced at once the two greatest cultural breakthroughs of history: Television and the hamburger.

I can recall two things about that night: The fabulous smell of burger patties and onions sizzling on the grill of that pokey burger joint, and the eighteen inch HMV television set, perched at an odd angle on the shelf. The Cisco Kid galloped across the black and white screen and held my mother and me transfixed as we stood in the doorway, gaping. We couldn't go in of course. Hamburgers and joints that served them were bad. We stood there for an hour.

The widow and her mite.

It would be another eighteen months before television and hamburgers would take a foothold in sleepy Adelaide where I lived.

Standards? What were they?

Hamburgers were sold out of dingy little ex-fish and chip shops and run by people who looked like they had not had a bath for a week. They smelled like they used onions for deodorant. (What was deodorant?) They wore white T-shirts and once-white aprons with gack splattered all over them. Their pasty-faced kids hung around in the shop in bare feet looking like they'd slept in their clothes and didn't know what a comb was. If they handed you your burger it was with hands they'd just coughed in or patted the dog with.

If you thought the egg wasn't cooked or the meat was raw, you ate it anyway and came back again next time hoping your luck might have changed. After all, it was the only burger shop for miles and the only one with a TV – and a juke box.

If you asked to use the toilet ... Wait! No-one asked to use the toilet.

Why not? I think there was less high fibre food in those days so you didn't need to go for a month. There was also less water to drink so you could go morning and night only.

But let's say you did need to use the facility – I think they were called lavvies in those days – you would have been laughed at. The only toilet was down the lane behind the shop behind the pepper tree. You tore pages out of the phone book for ... well you know what for.

Looking back you will recall that life was like that everywhere. You took what was dished up because that's the way things were. You put up with the bad-tempered butcher, the ignorant green grocer and the arrogant draper. They were part of the adventure called living. They were something to gossip about over the fence.

Then someone lifted the bar

That is all very different from today. Since those days it is not only the high jumpers and the pole vaulters who have to leap higher to qualify for competition. The bar has been raised for business too.

• You expect to use the 'bathroom' when you buy a hamburger. And it's clean! (so's the toilet!) When it's not you tell a pimply faced fifteen-year-old (who leaves his wet towel on the bathroom floor at home for his mother to pick up) and he races out with a mop and bucket and smartens it up for you. Land sakes they even let you have a birthday party on the premises in a special room and supply an ice cream cake and a clown!

• The butcher cuts up your meat and pops it on skewers. He marinates your chicken wings. Chicken! Once you only had chicken as a luxury for Christmas and gave the wings to Grandpa to gnaw on!

• The baker offers you two thousand five hundred varieties of baked products. Once, if the bread carter's horse was in a bad mood you had to chase the cart down the street for a choice of only white or brown or wait until tomorrow.

• The pharmacist sells you novels, book ends and computer games, when once you only went there if you were too sick to go to work and too poor to pay the doctor.

How did that happen?

It had been happening since the industrial revolution but a few things held it up. At times these large scale cataclysms even sped it up: Revolutions, colonisation, the American War between the States, the First and Second World Wars, influenza epidemics, polio epidemics, The Great Depression, oil discoveries, just to mention a few.

The historian Henry Adams noted in 1901 that the boy of 1854 stood closer to the year 1 than to the year 1900. That could also be said of the child of 1990 who stands closer to the year 1 than to the year 2000.

Just think.

- It took humans five thousand years to progress from the wheel to the steam engine and only a hundred to get from the steam engine to the moon.

- It took humans five thousand years to progress from the bow and arrow to the single shot musket and only one hundred to get from the Gattling gun to the plastic muzzled Uzi.

- It took humans five thousand years to progress from the message stick to the telephone and only one hundred years to the mobile network.

- It took humans five thousand years to progress from the smoke signal to the telegram and only one hundred from the telegram to e-mail.

Mechanisation, communication, modernisation and sophistication have been on the move for centuries but they all picked up speed in the last forty years and accelerated to break neck speed in the late eighties.

The fifties

The great influence was the bulge in the population in the fifties which precipitated massive shifts in western society. There were more people with more employment and more money. Creativity abounded. It was almost as if you could invent anything and it would become an instant success.

However there was no call for high standards. You simply built it, advertised it, sold it and banked the money.

Change was a wild bear stirring from a long sleep with a very empty stomach. He was getting ready to roar and wreak havoc.

The sixties

More competition emerged. Speed became an issue and the price and discount wars started. Big chain stores and supermarkets began to push the Neanderthals and locals aside.

Consumers became more mobile and would travel far and wide for bargains on daily necessities. The marketplace began to hold more competitors who could each still earn a living and choice became a luxury.

Quality was not an issue. Neither were manners. It was push, push,

push with price discounts, trade-ins and corny advertising urging mass consumerism.

The seventies

The smarter operators began to differentiate their stronger selling points. They racked their brains for enticing advertising slogans which would woo customers into buying but which in reality committed them to nothing.

Car dealers advertised 'production line reconditioning' on used cars – but sold cars that didn't have it. Electrical goods salespeople offered long warranties – but gave rise to marketplace cynicism in the phrase, 'not worth the paper they were written on'. Goods were produced in a hurry with no quality control, radical fashions were wiped out in a flash at the whim of the manufacturers, and built-in-obsolescence became the rule of thumb in manufacturing.
Cynicism against businesses was standard fare.

The eighties

Several things happened at once and made it impossible for mediocre businesses to survive.
Consumers became fed up – It would only be a matter of time before people tired of the chicanery of evil doers and slack artists. Television current event shows and talk back radio were filled with lurid tales of empty promises, exploitation and shoddy practices. Consumer Affairs departments were set up by governments to protect the population from crooks and con-artists. It was common knowledge and shoppers became defensive and suspicious.
Foreign manufacturers scared the locals – Japanese cars,

cameras and electronic good began to unsettle the waters of complacency. The people who had been famous for making cheap junk were storming through world markets with fabulous products. In the sixties the Honda 50cc motorcycle had been a cute little joke and their three-wheeled car had been a side splitter but twenty years had seen Japanese manufacturing dominate the world. The best cars were Japanese and then Korean and then Taiwanese. It was the same for televisions, radios, computers and watches.

American and European manufacturers and their retailers had to run to catch up. This contributed to a world-wide awareness of high standards and excellence in product and delivery. Mass education ushered in a time when everyone knew what quality was. Consumers had learned to be discerning and felt deserving. They began to get the upper hand.

Competition reached desperation point – More stores, more shopping centres, more malls and more products and services to choose from meant that the expendable dollar would have to be spread thinner. Smart retailers worked it out. They leaped at the opportunity to differentiate themselves. Speed of delivery became an issue. Rapid response to complaints became an issue. Hassle free exchanges became an issue. Delivering on promises became an issue. Even wearing smart uniforms and answering the phone became an issue. Just having a satisfying buying experience became an issue. Cluey business people were inventing ways to say, 'We can do it better so buy from us'.

The Neanderthals are to this day still stuck on price issues.

Bench mark companies settled in – British Airways, Scandinavian Airways, Volvo, Honda, Toyota, Sony, IBM, Apple, Boeing, McDonalds, Pizza Hut, Burger King (Hungry Jack's), Kentucky Fried Chicken, BP, AT&T, Chrysler, General Electric, all became known as world standard best practice operations.

They became the household name equivalent of success, image, good times and good value and became the standards against which others were measured. Most had been slowly building their empires over twenty or more years but they matured or reinvented themselves in the eighties.

Standards took on a life of their own.

And so today?

Today the trend continues. The coined word 'retailtainment' says it all. You must dazzle your customers. You must make them say, 'Wow'.

Raging, inexorable, thundering evangelists

You need to be a great big vacuum cleaner sucking them off the couch and into your store, where they beg you to take their money as they stand gasping for breath at the sheer exhilaration of buying from you.

Guy Kowasaki from Apple says we need to create raging inexorable thundering evangelists for our products or services. They should be gossiping hotly about you in the office, down at the bowls club, at bridge, at the football, in the school committee meetings and at church.

Is this you? I know you think it is far fetched and that the dosage for whatever medication I'm taking should be halved.

So I paint a big picture. Couldn't you live with it for a few minutes and imagine ways to make your customers desperate to be served by you?

Go on...

FIVE STAR IDEA:
List a few things that would thrill you if you were going to buy something from you.

LESSON 24

Git on Board li'l Chillun

It's been a long time since I heard the old spiritual but it comes a-rushin' back when I think of the pace of change in retailing...

> Git on board li'l chillun
> Git on board li'l chillun
> Git on board li'l chillun
> Or you'll be left behind.

Deciding is half the journey.

There is plenty of room for businesses who are willing to live by five star service. Those who don't rise to the call will be trampled in the rush of customers getting to the stores that have risen to it. Will you be one of them? It takes a decision now, not when you've finished the book, or even this lesson. Deciding is half the journey. Decide now. Say, 'Yes. I'll be counted among the winners and the stunners and the wowers! This book is about me and my attitudes.'

The record books are full of sad tales about businesses that have not made such a decision. They opted merely for survival, but didn't even do that. They decided on mediocrity – (the word means to be halfway up a mountain; medi - half, ocris - mountain) and choosing to venture no further up, they are back at the bottom today or completely out of business.

The ultimate disservice

Once household names these grand old emporiums have gone to the grave:

Marcus Clarke, McDonald and East, John Martin's, Broadway Stores, McDowells, Mark Foy, Prouds, Miller Anderson and far too many others. As a lad I never thought I'd see the day they would not be recognised by my own children but they performed the ultimate lousy service: They went out of business. Did the business fail? No the people failed the business.

Failure to adapt

Ten years after the change-over to decimal currency there was a store in a New South Wales country town that still displayed goods with price tags in pounds shillings and pence. It's not there today. Did the business fail? No the people failed the business. Will we be saying that of you because you failed to pick up a significant trend and adapt to it? Better technology for tracking customers and wider world access through the internet might be two to watch. Certainly keep your eye on everything in this book.

Failure to make money

As I write, the once famous Walton's store in Sydney has been a hole in the ground for eight years. Once a thriving business, its management failed to plug the leaks early enough and didn't have the skills to make it pump out profit. It was pulled down for lack of interest and the site has been a ghastly reminder that you can go from 'whole to hole' without leaving a trace. Did the business fail? No the people failed the business.

Failure to accept responsibility

This example is based on fact but the identities of the main players have been disguised to protect me from rocks through my window.

> There was a coffee shop in a prime location in a food court in a major shopping centre.
>
> As a long-standing successful business it was taken over by an inexperienced operator – someone who had no doubt merely bought herself a job. It began a sustained decrease in M.A.T. (Moving Annual Turnover) almost as soon as she took it over.
>
> It quickly fell below its break even point. The owner believed that this was wholly due to the lack of customers in the centre. There were in fact 130,000 customers a week. (A store like that ought to think of serving at least two percent of visitors. 2,600 customers spending an average of $4.50 is a good start to any store's figures at $11,700.)
>
> After continual complaints to the centre manager by the retailer, the centre management undertook an independent service audit on the retailer's business performance. Not surprisingly the audit results showed a score well below the sector average (ie for coffee shops) and considerably below the level suggested for best practice.
>
> Three separate results reflected scores of 32%, 46% and 30% for assessments in add-ons, cleanliness, promptness, smiling, and friendliness.
>
> Subsequent to this the retailer was offered both free consulting services and access to free retail training workshops to try and assist her business. A meeting between the retailer and the consultant took place from which an action plan and feasibility report was provided to the retailer.

After five months, not one action or recommendation was implemented by the retailer, no attendance was made by any staff member to any of the workshops, nor was any effort made to improve standards of customer service within the business.

All the while the whingeing, carping, whining, miserable blob of a retailer continued to complain to the centre management for the lack of customers.

After all this time, yet another three independent retail audits were undertaken on the business. The over-all rating for customer service and retail professionalism was still below 40% – bench marked against a sector average of 76%. The retailer refused to acknowledge that the service (or lack of it) had anything to do with her troubles and still blamed the centre, refusing to deal with any further consultants or retail trainers.

The centre had by this stage extended the 'usage clause' for the retailer and offered additional marketing support, however the retailer maintained a stance that the thousands upon thousands of potential customers who walked past her prime location, and didn't buy there any more, was purely because of the centre – not because of anything she was doing wrong - '... besides which' she said, 'customers probably just expected too much anyway'.

The business folded eighteen months after the take-over.

FIVE STAR IDEA:
Don't let your business appear as one of the examples in this lesson in future editions of this book. Get on board now. If this book does nothing else other than put you in a mind to ask for help and good advice then it has paid for itself another thousand times.

LESSON 25

Customers are worth a lot of money

You'd think from the rate at which some companies burn customers they were easy to come by and highly dispensable.

This is not so.
They cost a lot to get.
They spend a lot when you get them.
Their friends and families spend a lot on their recommendation.

They cost a lot to get

Customers don't just stroll in to your store because they have lost their way in the mall. Something made them want to come in.

Your advertising made them come in and that costs a lot

My Grandad Jim Cobbledick said 'There are two ways to lose money in business and advertising is both of them'.

Some advertising is a complete waste of money but if your advertising has been effective it has cost you a small fortune to stimulate Mr or Mrs Flubb to follow up on it. Say you spent $1,000 on some radio advertising and one hundred people responded. Each one cost you $10. If only ten responded, each response cost you $100. By letting those customers stroll in and stroll out without a greeting or a smile or an attempt to sell them something is as stupid as standing outside the mall and lighting people's cigarettes with $100 notes.

Your rent and store layout cost a lot of money

You chose your location and your store layout carefully because you understood the importance of store convenience and visual appeal. You wanted high foot traffic. That was a big financial decision. You ought to be consistent with yourself and run your current actions in line with what you then believed. Next time a customer walks in say to yourself, 'I'd best give this person five star service because they could help me pay the rent and for that flash sign at the front and this humungous display cabinet I'm slouching behind'.

Your stock and merchandising costs a lot of money

Need I explain? No. Everything you do in your store has one purpose: Sales; ie satisfying a customer's need through the supply of product. You spend wisely on stock and you are careful to merchandise it well. Your time and effort are a business expense. You do it all not simply to make the store look great but to make it throb and pulsate to the rhythm of passing customers' heart beats. If your aim was to attract them into your store, then surely it can't be too hard to work out that the mission is not accomplished until they are wooed, won and wowed with a sale.

Everything you do in your store has one purpose: Sales.

They spend a lot when you get them

Maybe the first time they come they only spend a few dollars; a bun from the baker or a second-hand tyre from the tyre retailer. The second time they come they spend more and so on they go for many multiples of visits.

Customers for life?

> A none too cheerful shopkeeper was finishing off a fight with a nasty and testy customer. The customer had mangled the product himself yet was blaming the shopkeeper for selling shoddy product. The shopkeeper was going to be no man's fool and promptly told the customer to take a long vacation in a warm place, but inferred he die first.
>
> As the customer left the shop in a rage, the shopkeeper called out after him, 'Anyway, I wish I had 1,000 more customers just like you'.
>
> Really shocked to hear what sounded like a complete reversal of form, the nasty customer blurted out, 'Why?'
>
> The answer was quick.
>
> 'Because at the moment I've got TWO thousand just like you!'

Do you want your customers for a lifetime?

Have you heard of the lifetime value of a customer? It's baloney in some ways because it is based on the almighty 'if'.

You can control your end of it. You can provide great service, great prices, great follow up, and great added value but the customers will only stay loyal if they are not wooed by the opposition or move states or get married to someone who hates you – or simply drop you because they couldn't care less.

But given that everything at your end is constant and your customer isn't a nut, yes you should expect to have that customer's money for life and you can calculate their value.

• Supermarkets figure that winning your loyalty is worthwhile. Say you live in an area for the average stay of seven years and you spend $200 on groceries every week. You'll spend $72,800 plus a few extras on festive occasions. At 20% average margin, you are worth $14,560 to them. If Grandma offered you $14,560 for being a good girl or boy, you could behave yourself for a while couldn't you? Truth is, there are several thousand such 'Grandmas' in the local catchment area and they are all worth keeping for their $14,560.

• Motor vehicle marketers have worked it out too. You keep your car on average for seven and a half years so that means in your lifetime you are up for at least eight cars. (I used my quota long ago). If they make about $1,500 on a car then you are worth about $12,000 all up. That's not much really so they figure you are worth nurturing for all your service, crash repairs and spare parts work. They figure services to be worth $1,500 in the first three years of ownership alone. And there's about $1,500 value on your trade-in. Now you are suddenly worth $36,000 for your total lifetime value. Worth offering five star service to you? You betcha.

Unfortunately many dealers haven't worked this out. They stitch you up for a car and then don't lock you into loving supportive service and attention. They either leave you to your own local mechanic or put you in the hands of spare parts, crash repair and service managers whom they breed in special pens at the bacon farm and whose brains would fit into a gnat's navel where there'd still be room left over for the finance manager's heart. (Thanks Mr Mark Twain.)

Activity: What is your customer worth in a lifetime?

First work out how often a customer buys your commodity – or a commodity like it from your opposition. _________

Now calculate the gross sale and the profit margin on each sale $ _____

Take the average stay in an area as seven years. Multiply that by the above two figures and there's your customer's value $_______

Their friends and families spend a lot on their recommendation

In the first book in this series, *Make More Money from Every Sale*, (Lesson 4) there is an exercise which helps you calculate the lifetime value of your customers and their circle of influence. Rather than repeat the exercise here I suggest you get hold of that book and complete it in the context of making more money from every customer. If you don't yet have the book, use the order form at the end of this one to get your copies.

I explain in '*Make More Money...*' that every one of us has a circle of influence of at least two hundred people, including relatives, friends, work colleagues, sports team members and all the spouses, kids and sweethearts – and *their* circles of influence in turn. That's a lot of people.

FIVE STAR IDEA:
Give five star service to every customer – even those you don't like – it's just simple business sense.

LESSON 26

YOU ONLY GET TO KEEP WHAT YOU GIVE AWAY

I must have slept through this lesson in kindergarten or Sunday School or Social Ed. I looked at my life the other day and realised how selfish it is and how bound up it is with getting, saving and banking and how little it has to do with giving.

I thank the publishers of Guideposts Magazine and the author Colleen Graham of Ashland, Oregon, for allowing me to abridge her true story. It appeared in the December 1997 issue.*

> One dreary snowy morning Pastor Colleen Graham was sitting in her church office wistfully longing for the warm days of Spring to hurry along.
>
> Interrupting her melancholy thoughts the church pianist, Marion Brown opened the door and shook some snow from her coat and took off her gloves. Flashing her customary impish smile she reached into her pocket and pulled out a large red shiny apple. 'For you', she said, 'to bring some colour into your life'.
>
> 'Where did you get such a beauty at this time of year?' the Pastor asked.
>
> 'A salesman travelling north gave it to me this morning for playing his favourite songs last night.' Marion lived in the local hotel and often played the piano in the lobby for the guests.
>
> Marion bundled herself off saying, 'I can't stay. I'm off to the

Kiwanis Club to play a few tunes to cheer them up. Then I'll be at the hospital to play in the ward later on.' Every organisation in town seemed to enjoy Marion's lovely gift of music.

Pastor Graham sat the apple on the desk as her first appointment for the day arrived. Steve, a young logger, was worried about his sister, Lucy, who was having her first baby. 'She's afraid she might lose it. This baby means so much to her and her husband ... and to all of us. Could you pray for her?'

As Pastor Graham closed her prayer the young man stood to leave and seeing the apple asked, 'Is that real?'

'Yes', she said and felt an urge to give it to him. 'Take it', she said. Steve protested but she urged him to take it and give it to Lucy as a reminder that Someone was caring for her and her baby.

A busy day followed and as the sun set, Pastor Graham set out for home. As she sat in her car waiting for it to warm up she saw a familiar figure making her way through the snow. It was Marion Brown.

'I've got to tell you about my day', she said and bustled herself into the front seat out of the chilly wind. 'I told you I was off to the hospital as I do every Wednesday. I play in the maternity ward and when I'm done I visit all the young mothers. The nurses told me about a young woman called Lucy who was feeling low. I called on her and she told me how her brother had visited and brought her a shiny red apple – just like the one I gave you this morning.'

Pastor Graham smiled.

'Her brother told her it was a special apple and would remind her that God was looking after her. She had laughed and the baby had jumped inside her. She'd told him it was an answer to her own prayers. But you'll never guess what happened next. She gave me the apple.'

Pastor Graham says she bit her tongue and revealed nothing.

Marion bubbled on, 'It's even more perfect than the one I gave you this morning. My husband will be so pleased because he hasn't been feeling the best himself lately and this will cheer him up.'

The apple had travelled its full circle.

Pastor Graham concludes her story saying,

'Gifts go far in the hands of giving people'.

If you've been to a funeral you've heard the words, 'Naked we come into the world, and naked we leave'. We spend our puny lifetime collecting mountains of stuff only to suffer the indignity of being stuffed in a box when it's over and buried without any of it. Nothing matters a cow pat except the legacy we leave from our love and good deeds and as the old book says, the treasure we store up in Heaven.

Truly you only get to keep what you give away.

Truly you only get to keep what you give away.

Activity: Write your epitaph. List the things you'd like said about what you stood for and what you contributed to the lives of others. Surely you wouldn't want it to read, 'Today we buried Bob who owned five shops, a boat, and had a great collection of antique gimbals. Missed by his dogs.'

Try answering these questions and see if you are happy with the result:

For what guerilla acts of kindness will you be missed?

For how many overlookings of the mistakes of others will you be remembered?

For what inspiring words of wisdom will you be noted?

For how many deeds of philanthropy will you be treasured?

Who will weep and why?

Who will stand to praise you the most and for what – your stuff, your personal achievements or your heart?

FIVE STAR IDEA:
Consider your life. Isn't living to give five star service one of the only things that will matter when everything is said and done.

LESSON 27

THE ICE CREAM BLOKE AND THE GELATI MAN

The Lovely Christine and I were taking a stroll at our favourite seaside resort accompanied by those two eating machines: the teenage twins, the devourers themselves, the unfillable, the unplugable, the undeterred by claims of parental poverty, privation and paucity.

'Ice cream!' they shouted as we came in whiffing distance of the ice cream shop. 'I smell ice cream!' their little curly tails were whirling like propellers.

The ice cream stores know that ice cream doesn't smell so they invented this great marketing idea: Make the sugar cones on site so customers are attracted by the delicious aroma of toasting cones. You can smell it for fifty metres up the street.

Only a handful of retail products sell by the olfactory sense. The list isn't much longer than leather, chocolate, perfume, roasted nuts, cookies, bread, coffee, and at the repulsive end – fish. Ice cream is on the strictly anosmic end of the smell spectrum. But boy oh boy those cones are right up the 'yum-yum' end.

So here we are approaching the ice cream shop and they already had their trotters in their mother's purse. They leant over the glass counter poking, pointing and giggling like greedy two-year-olds – actually like greedy fourteen-year-olds.

Two of the three staff were preoccupied with something going on in the back room and the other one looked like she had just been dropped by her boyfriend, so I tried to distract the herd and tell them that the shop along the road a way was a much better shop but they were already dribbling down their shirts.

'Gimme a cookies and cream and a banana honey crunch', and then after a kick from me, 'Oh yeah! – Please. Snort! Snort!'

'And I want a choc almond fudge and a hazelnut whirl – PLEASE', says Greedy Pig No 2.

Duly served without a sign of life, we parted with our money and the porkers started a war over how much of their snouts they could get into the other's pile of ice cream. That kept them occupied until we reached our favourite shop.

My favourite ice cream man looked at the boys' ice creams and then at me in disgust. 'Look', he said, 'they don't even cook their cones properly.'

'Here let me put a new one around yours. It's cracked!' he said to Greedy Pig No 1, and to the other one he said, 'Here, you need more caramel topping than that on their Hazelnut whirl. It's tasteless.' With that he slopped on a dollop of topping to the delight of GP#2.

Then to me he said, 'So how about a taste of something?'

'OK', I said, 'I'll try a lick of mocha

Try a sample.

swirl and a bit of macadamia coffee.' The Lovely Christine skipped the trial and went straight for the kill. 'Vanilla and strawberry please', she begged. So adventurous!

'And how about I bribe you into coming here first next time. Have a topping on the house. Chocolate, strawberry or caramel?'

'Yes please', I said.

Without a blink on went all three.

I asked, 'You must have been reading my book, '*Make More Money from Every Sale*' have you?'

'No', he said.

'Well I'm kidding because it isn't out yet', I said. 'Three weeks.'

'Well when it's out send me one. Here's my address.'

Then he wrote out his address on the back of a two-for-one voucher.

'Use it next time', he said.

As we walked on I drilled the two little pigs on the simple wonders of business success.

Later as we strolled up the footpath opposite, we came across the gelati store. For some reason the guy recognised me and called me over.

Business wasn't good he told me. 'Customers don't understand that

Gelati is better. How come no-one wants any?

gelati isn't made with water.'

I asked him where his cone maker was along with his olfactory factor.

'I hate the smell of those cones', he said. 'In Italy we buy with our eyes so I have a great display of gelati.'

'Well what about your two-for-one vouchers and your taste spoons?'

'You can't keep giving away your profits', he bragged.

There only seemed to be one problem. They were still lined up at the ice cream bloke's shop but there was not a customer in sight (or smell) of the gelati shop.

Five Star Idea:
Get it. Five Star Service is being awake, being interested in your customers, being pro-active about sales, being alert – and as you know there just aren't enough lerts these days.

SECTION 4

How to give five star service on a one star budget

Ready to go?
By now you should be bursting with anticipation of creating a widly successful five star service culture.

LESSON 28

START WITH THE RIGHT PEOPLE

Why do store owners start with locating a site, getting products, laying out the store, do their slick merchandising, and smart advertising and then hire the people last? Somehow they hope they'll be the lucky ones who fluke a team of people who instinctively do the right thing.

It doesn't happen. You have to scour the earth for the right people. The right people need to have five things going for them:

1. They have to love people
2. They must be active
3. They must be willing to serve
4. They must be outgoing
5. They must have non-discriminatory attitudes about other people - sex, race, religion, age.

1. They have to love people

The National Retail Training Council commissioned a survey of customers and managers so that they could establish ideal selection criteria for salespeople.

Customers and managers were asked to rank the desirable characteristics of salespeople.

The No. 1 spot was grabbed by 'Basic liking for others – a genuine love for people'. Not product knowledge; not the ability to close hard and fast; not negotiating skills; but good old-fashioned friendliness: friendliness in tone and word and deed.

A warm-hearted manner seems the most fundamental secret for success in business.

Confucius say:
He who cannot smile, should not keep shop!

How does the song go?

> What the world needs now, is love sweet love.
> That's the only thing that there's just too little of.

It's an easy tune to hum in a karioke bar with warm wishes for Africans to stop shooting each other for Christmas, but putting up with customers is another matter.

• Loving the Hoochoos in Africa is somehow easier than loving a customer whose hair colour ran down her face in the rain blaming you for selling something with tiny instructions.

• Loving your neighbour as much as you love yourself is really easy provided your neighbour isn't an angry customer whose dress split open on the dance floor when you said it was a perfect fit.
It might help if you look at your customers as if they are in pain - not A pain – but in pain.

Most people are in pain about something: A wayward child, a strained relationship, a family quarrel, a lover's spat, a nasty neighbour, a terminally ill parent, a drug or alcohol dependent friend or relative, a bad report, and right at the top of the list – not enough money to do what they really want to do. There's a lot of pain out there.

Treat your customers as though they could be in pain and do what you can to ease it. You'll be amazed at the response.

This appeared in my Bright Ideas Newsletter one Christmas:

> I was hungry and you sat around the lunch table and felt guilty about having so much to eat while you discussed my hunger. Thank you.
> I was imprisoned and you rang up talk back radio and said I should have been hanged. Again, thanks.
> I was robbed and left naked and you made smart alec remarks in the staff canteen about how much better I'd look in a sexy dress. Appreciated.
> I was sick and you hugged your kids closer and hoped they wouldn't catch it from me. Fair enough.
> I was homeless and you said there were plenty of shelters for people like me and muttered something about finding a job. Good advice.
> I was lonely and you walked past with your friends and didn't stop to say hello. I suppose you thought I would bite you for loose change. I guess I would have.
> You seem so good; so well dressed; so well bred; so together; so

deserving of all the good things that have happened to you. And I don't mind that. I don't want to take it away from you. You're OK the way you are.

But I'm still very hungry, and lonely, and cold.

FIVE STAR IDEA:
Choose team members who love a little more. It's not an accident of the emotions. It's an act of the will.

2. They must be active

A dull-headed and unpresentable youth applied for a job.

He didn't want to work in the factory because he got a rash on his hands from grease. He didn't want to work in the grounds because he got hayfever from grass. He didn't want to work on deliveries because he got stressed from working to deadlines. He didn't want to work in sales because the love of money is the root of all evil.

The interviewer, painfully aware of equal opportunity legislation and knowing he couldn't reject the lad just because he was

> unemployable said, 'What this company really needs is a good professional worrier. Young man, can you sit behind that desk every day and worry in a constructive manner?'
> The young man said, 'What does the job pay?' The employer answered, '$600 a week'. 'Fine', said the applicant, 'I'll take the job and be the best worrier you ever saw. By the way, who pays me the $600?'
> 'That', said the interviewer, 'is your first worry'.

In the survey the customers and managers listed an Active Style as the second most important attribute of sales team members.

George Bernard Shaw believed in action. He said,

> People are always blaming their circumstances for what they are. I don't believe in circumstances. The people who get on in this world are the people who get up and look for the circumstances they want, and if they can't find them, make them.

Action elicits a reaction. The more positive the action, the greater the chance of eliciting a positive reaction.

> I was in Melbourne for lunch with a friend and walking through Collins Plaza we were arrested by a little bloke outside his cafe with a cloth over his arm. 'You wanna lunch?' he asked, expecting the answer yes, and motioning us inside. We followed like little lost lambs and sat down at our table as if it had all been pre-booked.

That's making life happen to you, the way you prefer it.

You can never build your success or your reputation on what you're going to do.

Your customers need to see you making things happen. If you are in retail, they want to see you darting about and looking busy with customer affairs – not frantic mind you, just busy.

Edward Bok thought that the three really great things in the world are a mountain, the ocean and an earnest person at work – the potentiality of each are beyond human calculation.

We're all aware of the fact that in this life there are people who make things happen, people who watch things happen, and people who are never aware that anything happened at all. The only people who make a contribution to the world and its citizens are the people who make things happen.

> I met a chap yesterday who had closed his car repair business for an hour or two and had come out on the rounds looking for car parts. He had no message machine, no mobile telephone and no interest in getting new customers. 'I've got enough', he said. Maybe he does.
>
> He is single. He is happy. He has enough and he is not greedy. But he is not taking his responsible place in the food chain. He is not employing. He is not teaching his immense skills to younger people. He is not letting other people enjoy his special talents and high levels of customer service. He has buried himself in a cosy corner where he won't get damaged.

FIVE STAR IDEA:
Be seen to be active. Throw yourself into your work. It's what the customer wants to see.

3. Be a servant

You can't overlook these characteristics when you are hiring new staff. It's dumb to hire people because they look nice or have great qualifications or boast long experience. If the basic building blocks are missing then everything else is smoke.

The English verb: to sell, has its roots in the Norwegian verb: *selje*: to serve. It's probably how phrases about 'being served' came into the language of retail.

Selling by nature has deep connotations of servanthood about it. To be successful in sales and therefore successful in business we have to see ourselves as servants. (In case you think I don't know how often I bring this up, I've been counting. This is the third time I've beaten this drum in the book.)

This hurts most people to whom I spell it out. The idea of being someone's servant is anathema to 99% of the salespeople I train. That's why they need training! They just don't get it. When they applied for their job they thought they were applying for a pay packet. The person who employed them neglected to ask if they understood that they were entering a life of servitude. It's like receiving a calling.

This is why customer service is such a hot topic. Over the last few frenzied decades we've lost touch with the heart of it.

Customer Service – ie being customers' servants, is the root stock on which all branches of healthy sales grow: Add-on sales, repeat sales, referral sales, and long-lasting customer relationships.

Think about how you like to be treated when you are the customer. We walk out our front door each morning wearing a sandwich board which reads,

> Notice me,
> the centre of the universe,
> the nicest person in the world,
> the only person I think about from dawn till dusk.

This is the cruncher. Business is the playing field where our own desire to be served meets the need to serve others. Here we are sitting at our desk, pushing a mower, fitting a tyre, answering a phone, working behind the counter wearing our 'notice me, love me, serve me' sign and we are confronted by another person wearing the same sign.

This is what we have come to know in customer service studies as 'the moment of truth'.

We have to take off our sign and turn it around so it reads:
'I notice you. I love you.
I'm here to be your servant.'
The Great Storyteller said, 'He who would be greatest among you must humble himself and be servant of all'.
It's a tough one.

> I don't know what your destiny will be, but one thing I know; the only ones among you who will be really happy are those who will have sought and found how to serve.
>
> *Dr Albert Schweitzer*

FIVE STAR IDEA:
Start a discussion among your colleagues about what being a servant means in your business. It will sort out the dead wood almost instantly.

4. They must be outgoing

Business and particularly retailing is a Punch and Judy Show.

Right now there's a bloke on my roof looking at the air conditioning unit. You can probably hear him thumping around in his iron shoes. He's the third bloke we've had look at it in two years. I have this silly idea that air conditioning is supposed to make you cool but every summer ours slowly roasts us.

So we get a bloke to come. Each bloke is a disappointment so we save up and try another one.

Do they have a special school for air conditioning blokes where they teach them to be grunters, nongs, and drongos?

I reckon they do, because no-one is born that way.

As I see it these must be the rules for running an air conditioning business.

- Run a big ad in the Yellow pages so no-one thinks you are a nong.
- Answer the phone like you're on the way to the potty.
- Arrive on the job looking like you just got out of the St Vinnie's old clothes bin.
- Have grubby mitts.

- Chew gum with your mouth open.
- When the people answer the door say, 'Bout the egg nishner. You called up.'
- Grunt at every question and defensively imply that the customer is trying to blame you for their hot house even though you never met them before.

Hello out there. Listen up for your own good.
This is your old Uncle Colin telling you this because he cares.
Every employee who meets your customers is a salesperson
– Not a trades person
or a rep
or a clerk
or a receptionist
or a tech
or a supervisor
or a *shop assistant*

They are ALL salespeople.
If I don't buy *them* I don't buy *you*!
Is this getting through?
I don't think so.
They give business licences to anyone these days!

Great sales people (and therefore reps and tradespeople and techs etc...) exhibit all five of these not-so-spectacular characteristics.
Along with the first three characteristics retail team members need a sense of theatre about them.
They need to smile and spread a bit of joy – even on hot days. Like

a Punch and Judy show they come out in their funny hats and dance around to entertain the crowd. The crowd is pleased and comes back the next day and throws even more money in the tin.

My Mum used to get a plumber who whistled while he worked and a painter who sang to himself. It was worth having them around for the pleasure of their company.

When was the last time you heard anyone whistle, sing or laugh on the job?

The one thing I love about my job is that I am surrounded by garrulous laughter. The two Chrises who work with me giggle their fat little heads off many times a day, and the people in my seminar audiences get a good laugh too.

Everywhere else, it looks like life's turned into a funeral dirge. It seems everybody's worked out that they are going to be dead for an awfully long time so they are putting in a lot of practice now to get it right when the time comes.

Sam Walton, founder of the Walmart empire and the richest man in America in the eighties said this about his success from his college days.

> I learned early on that one of the secrets to campus leadership was the simplest thing of all: speak to people coming down the sidewalk before they speak to you.

FIVE STAR IDEA:
Get your people to come up with ways they can be more outgoing.

5. They must have non-discriminatory attitudes about other people - sex, race, religion, age etc...

People...Ugh!!!

> Lucy in the Peanuts cartoon shouts indignantly
>
> 'I love the world. It's the people I hate!'

That's great for Lucy to have the freedom to hate people. She's just a kid in the funny papers. In sales there is just no room for that kind of attitude.

I guess it follows that if you have the first four characteristics, you are unlikely to fail at the fifth, but you never know. You might not have been honest with yourself over the first four.

Just to keep tabs on it let's run an eye over some common prejudices. Check the list and see if you have ever, or do currently hold someone at arm's length over any of them.

Do you give out bad vibes to customers because of their:

Age
Body odour
Clothing - brand
Clothing - condition
Clothing - style
Disability - Mental
Disability - Physical
Employment status
Gender bias
Hair - colour
Hair - lack of it
Hair - over supply

Hair - style
Intelligence - too little
Intelligence - too much
Nationality
Perfume/Cologne
Race
Religion
Sex
Size – Height - tall or short
Size – Weight – fat or thin
Skin colour
Social rank
Speech – accent
Speech – affectation
Speech – impediment
Speech – non English speaker
Spending power
Temperament

My guess is that you might have fared as badly on the list as I did. We are habitual discriminators. So how can we ask new applicants to miss out on sales positions because they are like the rest of us? Good question. It comes down to this:

Most of us acknowledge our prejudices and work hard to overcome them. Others licence themselves to hold hard attitudes against certain groups or individuals in the community. If you employ these haughty individuals they will ruin your business and your reputation.

When you're interviewing them, ask if they have any problems on the check list. If they do, ask them probing questions to discover whether they will cause your customers any problems if you employ them. If they fail this test, don't employ them.

I meet a lot of sales people in my work. Most of them are really nice people. But there's a big bunch of pompous know alls – there I go discriminating again – who have squeezed through the net, just because they were good-looking, or smart, or went to the right school.

In the final analysis, they will betray themselves but unfortunately you never really know how much they have betrayed you in the meantime.

FIVE STAR IDEA:
Be nice to someone outside your comfort zone today. Commit a random act of kindness.

LESSON 29

Develop a Cheerful returns policy

You MUST guarantee satisfaction

If you can't guarantee satisfaction you should quickly ring your museum and buy yourself a spot on the fossil shelf. That's the only place you'll be useful as time catches up with you

Bad press

Next Christmas when you are showing off your new gismo and bragging to your brother-in-law about its reliable track record and huge reputation, you will throw in one last desperate proof line to show you are an astute buyer.

'And it's guaranteed', you'll say.

'Pah!' He'll scoff, 'Guarantees aren't worth the paper they're printed on'.

This is the fossil department children. Here's where we keep the retailers who would not exchange goods.

Why are guarantees 'useless'?

How do people get the impression that guarantees are worthless? I guess it's because in the past guarantees have been a con job. The guarantees were full of loop holes and by-laws that protected the manufacturer or retailer from unscrupulous customers who were careless with the product and then expected the business person to wear the cost.

I know that there are more rip-off artists in the market place posing as hard-done-by customers than there are among business people. The 6.30pm current affairs programs would have you believe otherwise. They make you feel like a real 'low-life' just for opening a shop.

These questions plague retailers

Should I give the money back on unsatisfactory goods?
Should I accept returned product?
Should I accept returned product without a receipt?

I guess this is the most emotive issue I raise with my clients. Join the party. I expect this to be a debate that will rage for many years to come. Let's see if we can get satisfactory closure on this in the next five minutes.

Why wouldn't you have a cheerful returns policy?

I have summarised the myriad of responses into four categories:

It messes up your bonus
It hurts
People take advantage
It costs too much.

Let's put some thought into this. Can you stop holding your breath and turning blue so we can have a rational discussion for a minute? Stop it. Your forehead will blow a vein.

It messes up your bonus

> Graeme Maher told me how he visited a large and well-known department store in New York which was supposed to be legendary for its cheerful returns policy.

He was the first customer of the morning and presented a bottle of expensive perfume which he'd bought for his wife in one of their other stores in Los Angeles. Since buying the perfume he'd begun to think he'd gone a little overboard on the one item and felt he should get more gifts for his money. 'I've changed my mind about this', he said, 'I bought it in one of your other stores. I'd like to get a refund but I might get something else to go with it.'

'A refund?' said the salesperson, obviously annoyed. 'What a way to start the day. I'll never catch up! Hey Bob', she said to her colleague, 'Look at this. A return first thing in the morning. Don't that roast your chicken!'

Equally miffed, the colleague said, 'A refund! You'll never catch up your figures for the day!'

'Is there a problem?' asked Graeme.

'Can't you take it back to where you bought it?'

'It was on the West Coast.'

He suggested they call the department head. Graeme repeated that he wanted to get a refund but would like to buy something else. The department head was nearly as disturbed as the other two.

'You know, you should be treating this as an opportunity for an add-on sale', Graeme told them. 'I've told you twice I want to buy something else. You should be focusing on that.'

You get lumped with a dud

It seemed to Graeme as though their bonus was at stake. Many commission structures work on this basis. No matter who handles the return or refund the company applies a penalty to the daily figures of the poor salesperson who gets lumped with it. If it happens near the close of a month or at the end of a contest it can be heart breaking when it means dropping to a lower bonus percentage point or missing out on a prize.

I've been over this one many times. For some managers it has to be this way because if it were not so their system would be open to abuse.

You've met salespeople who will win sales contests by selling anything to anyone, even signing up their dead grandmother, and then once the bonus is paid or the trip taken, half the sales fall through or come back as refunds. I've even come across dirt bags who've calculated how to earn a bonus on shaky sales making sure to point out that the best time for returns is at a time when they are not rostered on duty. There is only one way to fix this: Termination.

This has made retailers shy away from bonuses altogether but that is not the best answer.

Build in an extra reward

The best answer is to reward cheerful refund behaviour. Rather than penalise the person who gets stuck with the refund, build in a bonus for doing it. Isn't that obvious? Rather than subtract the figures from their score, add to them. You'll have team members rushing to handle refunds.

Build in an even bigger bonus for converting a refund to a larger order and stand back so you're not trampled in the rush to comply.

Naturally there will be the two clowns who will create a way for one to sell something to his cousin for the sales bonus while the other one scores on the refund bonus five minutes later.
And how do you deal with it? Easy. Call the Police.

Remember what the bonus is for

The second best answer is that the fair minded manager should take into account the brilliant salesperson whose final result was despoiled by refunds. Only a complete dope would set up a bonus system designed to not pay out because of petty failures. The very purpose of bonuses is to encourage Five Star Service behaviour. Go out of your way to reward it. It's part of your own Five Star Service philosophy that you are generous to your team isn't it? Isn't it?

You can't let it lie

The worst suggestion is that everyone should learn to live with the problem. This is crazy thinking. You can't expect the team to be so altruistic as to provide Five Star Service all day every day just because Colin Pearce wrote in his book that they should. We'd both be dreaming. The team needs encouragement. You have to create rewards and systems.

It hurts

Many retail staff tell me they hate giving the money back or replacing the product.
It's not just the bonus or the day's takings that are at stake. There is something in all of us that makes us feel defensive of our company, our product, and the way we sold it.
We know we didn't go out of our way to be dishonest or to sell a

shoddy product, yet when confronted by a disgruntled customer, whether the claim is dubious or not, we feel our personal integrity is being attacked.

It feels like a defeat.

No-one likes to lose. We feel like scoring one for the home team so we get into 'pay backs'. Some salespeople argue or start a fight. Some salespeople wouldn't dare be so rude so they just pull a face or make a catty remark. You hear them relating the story later. 'That showed her!' you'll hear them say.

We've all heard horror stories like this one.

> It was one minute past opening time on a Monday morning.
>
> The salesperson's eyes were barely open and there was not a soul in the shopping centre except for the night cleaners and the security guards drinking their coffee at the end of their shift.
>
> A big red-faced bully of a customer stormed into the salesperson's little store and banged a pair of shoes on the counter. 'I wanna refund! Last Friday you told my wife these would fit me and they don't. You're an idiot.'
>
> Flabbergasted, knowing that he had been at university on that Friday, the salesperson said the first thing that came into his mind. 'But I wasn't working here on Friday. It was the other sales guy.'
>
> 'No it was you alright. She described you to me. She came in and asked for a size 10 and these are size 9. I can tell. I tried to play basketball in them on Saturday and they nearly crippled me.'
>
> 'Well I'm sure Steve would have measured your feet. That's our policy.'

> 'Stop trying to get out of it mate! I wasn't here. It was my wife and you lied to her about the size so give me my money.'
>
> It was by this time painfully obvious that the salesperson was only going to be a victim.
>
> 'I haven't got enough money in the cash drawer. We only just opened and I've only got forty dollars for small change. Can you come ba...'
>
> Shouting now, the bully yelled, 'Listen here. I can get you at Consumer Affairs for this. I know my rights. I want the refund – $140.'
>
> 'B..b..but There's no money. I can't. I can give you another pair of shoes that fit better.'
>
> 'No.' The language from here on in the story is unprintable as he poured out a tirade of abuse. 'Give me my refund.'
>
> Finally in a stroke of desperate genius the sales person remembered his personal household rent money and shaking like a leaf he fumbled in his wallet and handed it over as the thankless customer stormed out.
>
> The salesperson spent the rest of the morning sitting in the stock bay shivering and crying.

The story is true. The pain is still real to the salesperson many years later.

Yes. It hurts.

Even if you have not experienced trauma like that, you sometimes know the humiliation of having to take back a returned product. It is therefore no surprise to me that many salespeople and business owners have built up a barrier against experiencing that hurt by not having a Cheerful Refunds Policy.

It's time to get over it!

Some people are dishonest

There are crooked and immoral people out there who see shop keepers as fair game. They equate you with major corporations that make billions of dollars and mindlessly assuage their guilt by assuming you can afford their dishonesty.

• They steal product from a store that stocks similar product to yours and 'return' it at your store telling you that they lost their receipt.

• They buy product at another store on a credit card and 'return' it at yours for a cash refund, never intending to pay the credit card bill.

• They bring product back months after its normal life is over when it is worn out or broken from abusive wear and tear. They tell you the product was faulty and that you are obliged to replace it.

• In claiming their refund for damaged stock, they lie about how the product was damaged, claiming faulty workmanship as the cause when in fact their own carelessness broke it.

• They use you as a lending library for fashion wear. They 'buy' a product in a Friday, wear it to a party on a Saturday and return it on a Monday claiming they changed their mind about it, swearing that they didn't wear it, and that the big perspiration stain under the sleeve was there when they bought it.

This makes most retailers hopping mad and they feel affronted by the crass roguery of these villains. In order to stamp it out, the retailers build a bastion of resistance to all refunds and post signs all over their stores announcing their counter measures.

It costs too much

There is an argument that says refunds cost the store owner too much and that if let get out of hand could ruin profitability and in some cases threaten viability. Thus a strict set of rules is posted and the staff drilled to treat all refunds with stiff resistance.

If the truth be known, this is just a cover up for the pain of the other three. It messes up bonuses, it hurts, and creates a desire to stamp out evil doers and knowing that none of these seems arguable in the cold light of day, retailers invent a reason that looks legitimate. *Cost becomes the cover for indignation.*

Stop it! It's ridiculous. It doesn't cost much at all. Ask anyone who has run with a cheerful returns policy for a long time and they will tell you that it has won them more business than it has cost them. I cited Graeme Maher's story from New York earlier because Graeme knows the refund business backwards. As part-owner of the one hundred and thirty nine strong chain of Suzanne Grae women's fashion stores he offers us this advice:

'Yes, you could relate case after case of people taking advantage of your "cheerful refund" policy but we never treated it as a cost to the business. We saw it as a small part of the deal.

You develop such enormous credibility.

We came out of Woolworths who taught us the value of a refund policy – mostly on low priced items – so we decided to implement it for apparel. It created huge goodwill. In those days in country towns all over New South Wales women might have only come to town once a month. They knew they could order garments and send them back in the mail if they were not happy with them. More than anything else that policy helped us get enough credibility to get the chain started.

Today I won't shop with a store that doesn't have a refund policy.

There is only one policy you can have: A cheerful refunds policy. And then you keep your sense of humour tucked up your sleeve.

FIVE STAR IDEA:

1. Choose to sell only products and services that are guaranteeable.

2. Send guarantees as a love note to your customer, saying 'Thank you for buying from me. Come back again, bring your friends and buy more.'

3. Do what the guarantee says – and then some. Give a $5 coffee and muffin voucher as well as a full cash refund when the customer is unhappy with the product.

LESSON 30

Post your service promise

Post your service promise

Go back to Lesson 18 and review the service promise you worked out.

Working it out is a good step but it's only the first of many. Now you have to work out how you will let customers know what you're promising. Will you display it, advertise it, slip it in with delivery dockets or print it on your stationery?

Why tell the customers?

Some people argue with me about whether to make their service promise known. When you tell your customers what you're promising, you achieve several things:

- You tell them they are special; so special in fact that you thought about them in advance and defined your relationship.
- You remind customers that you do things in a unique and wonderful way. They weigh this up when they think about taking their business elsewhere.
- You keep yourself and your team on your toes. You have to live up to your promise when you make it known.
- You define the limits of your service for the few who want your soul as well as your service.

Post your service promise and live by it

I reckon you should put it everywhere.

Let's say your grocery store promises to have no more than four people in a waiting line before you open a new service point.

Advertise it on TV and other media: *No waiting. No long queues.*

Make it into a press release: *In a bold new move, Uncle Colly's has set up a monitoring system to cut down waiting time for grocery shopping ...*

Put up placards: *If you're in a line with more than four people waiting, start chanting, 'New queue, New queue'.*

Print it on the receipts: *It's not the Great Depression. We believe you shouldn't have to stand in line to buy groceries.*

Print badges for the team: *We're not sorry for keeping you waiting. We just don't do it!*

Put up an effigy of a checkout person in the stocks with a caption: She had a line with five people in it.

Activity: Work out how to make your service promise known. Choose the means and the time lines under which you will operate to get this done.

Live by your service promise. Don't die by it

A store advertised a promotion whereby if the salespeople didn't say 'Thank you' at the conclusion of a transaction, customers could mention the fact and be awarded a $5 cash rebate.

A man passed through the checkout without receiving the obligatory 'Thank you' from the operator and asked, 'Haven't you forgotten something?'

'Forgotten what?' asked the operator.

'You didn't say, "Thank you" so I'd like to cash in on my $5 rebate.'

'Sorry,' said the operator, 'but that promotion finished last week.'

That shows you the difference between a shallow promotional gimmick and a real service promise. In a real service promise the team would have to live by such a promise regardless of the date.

I popped into a restaurant with another business consultant where they were advertising a lunchtime 'special' whereby the food would be served in ten minutes or it would be free. We were more interested in the food than the 'free' and would not have noticed the mess they made of it if they had not decided to die by their own hand.

It was supposed to be a working lunch. We hardly took any notice of the waitress because we were already into deep discussion about the advertising campaign we were writing. We ordered off the menu and got back to work.

As the waitress departed she plonked a timer on the table already running. Our focus now shifted to the timer, totally and thoroughly transfixed by the need to catch her out if she were not back with our meal in ten minutes.

The ten minutes came and went and at around twelve and a half minutes the food arrived, hot, tasty and just as we had ordered it – but late.

We turned the clock around toward her and smugly tapped the dial.

'Oops!' she grinned. 'Lucky you. Sorry about that!'

We tucked in feeling very pleased with ourselves and then she came back with an I'm-having-the-last-laugh look on her face. 'The manager says that the offer only applies to the ten minute specials on the back of the menu and you ordered your meals off the front so you can't have them free. Orright?'

We looked at each other with a smirk and a wag of our heads.

'Would you like dessert or coffee?'

'Yes', we chorused, 'but not here.'

And we've never been back.

What went wrong? It was such a nice advertising gimmick. Yes it was, but it was not born out of a genuine service promise so when the crunch was on they couldn't carry through. The waitress had forgotten to point out the rules so the customers copped one in the eye.

They were good rules by the way. I love that kind of thinking. Bulk order and pre-cook four or five dishes and whoosh the customers through. Make lots of money and look impressive. You can do it in under five minutes but you keep them waiting nine just to add a little theatre and run panting to the table as if you were really anxious about it. Every now and then you run over by half a minute and someone gets a free meal with the ringing of loud bells to attract attention to your 'mistake'. Out of sheer sympathy for you they order more drinks. Wonderful retailing.

But this has little to do with a long-term philosophical promise of fast and accurate service.

Activity: Cover all your bases. Make sure your service promise is understood by every team member and that no-one misunderstands or has a maverick approach.

Exceed your service promise

If you want to create a truly memorable impression, simply exceed your promise.

- Do you promise twenty-four hour turnaround time on your orders? Send the orders gift wrapped or include a handful of chocolates too.
- Do you promise your phone will be answered by a person and not one of those infernal computerised people bluffers? Have your team answer in three rings and with a huge smile and a great greeting as well.
- Do you promise that your eye glasses frames are guaranteed

Sauce with your pie?

for twelve months? Offer to clean, check and adjust them any day of the week.

- Do you promise your plants will live for thirty days? Offer a sachet of liquid fertiliser too.

Warning!

Something strange will happen and it might annoy you so I'm giving you fair warning.

After you've provided the extra service a few times, customers will merge it with your promise and expect the extras every time 'because you promised' – even though you didn't; even though you did it as a treat. In being fairly warned you can prepare for it in two ways:

Don't perform 'extras' in a way that you won't be able to sustain when they are expected as a 'norm'.

Have a new 'extra' up your sleeve for the time when your old 'extra' becomes absorbed into the expectation inherent in the promise.

Activity: 1. Plan your strategy for exceeding your promise and 2. Plan your back up strategy for when your current excesses become the 'norm'.

FIVE STAR IDEA:
Promise a lot and over-deliver.

LESSON 31

Excellence! Phooey!

'We're thinking about developing an excellence policy', said the voice on the telephone. 'We're wondering if you can get us started with a seminar.'

I tried not to laugh. He was thinking about getting into something that had been going on since the sixties. It became vogue in the eighties. Here he was in the early nineties 'thinking' about it. My response was strong and to the point.

'Too late for an excellence policy! You need a Wow! policy, or a knock 'em-dead policy, or a suck-'em-off-their-couches policy, or a leave-'em-gasping-on-the-floor-for-breath policy, or a turn-yourself-into-a-legend-at-the-bowls-club policy.

I might have been a little rough on him because I still haven't heard from him again after six years.

We have a great Christmas card list

So does Santa and he's not real either.

Do you come from the school that thinks a pre-printed card at Christmas and birthdays is great customer service? It's a pleasant little thought but it is about fifty years behind the times as an idea. If I'm on your list, save yourself a dollar and cross me off. I think it's silly. When I get your Christmas card – (or your boring Christmas letter about your family!) – I yawn and click on the trash icon. Ask yourself this: If your accountant does it, is it really a great idea?

Love me for eleven months of the year and forget about Christmas unless you're sending me a really nice gift. And don't send wine. I'm a wowser and proud of it.

So I'm behaving hysterically. I know. I know. But you see most people need a snowball down their neck to wake them up. Loving your suppliers and customers once a year with a stupid picture of a fat bloke stuck in a stove pipe isn't stunning five star service. It's a waste of a really nice tree. If you're religious, you need to send people your love and prayers when their world is falling apart at tax or stocktaking time, not at Christmas.

Five Star service is perpetual. It's hard work. It requires attention to detail. It's beyond excellence. Here are five examples of people venturing beyond excellence into 'Holy Toledo, Batman!'

1. Hairdresser gets a raise of $1350 a year

Knowing she was on a short wicket with my receding hairline my hairdresser could see she needed a new revenue source if she was going to get money out of me long term.

So she introduced me to the neck and shoulder massage.
Yes, the leave-me-on-the-floor-gasping-for-breath neck and shoulder massage starring the long fingered Lisa!

I go in for my appointment with my head feeling like a mallee root cocky-wired to a lump of mulga and come out an hour later like a clown face on a rubber stick. The joy lasts a week and then I go back.

I reckon it's good value at $25 a pop, and I get to keep my shirt on! I'm sending the lovely Christine now too.

I just remembered, Marge. Are you coming bowling on Saturday night?

It wasn't a hard sell. The first one was free! I was hooked at the first touch.

Was it worth giving one away?

$1350 extra in annual revenue says, Yes!

2. A list of extras

I was sitting on a plane with Brad Cooper (Chief Executive of FAI Home Security) and he told me that when you get an FAI home security unit the installer follows a 40 point WE CARE checklist. Points 1 to 28 cover the installation as you'd expect it to be done. Points 29 to 40 create what Brad calls 'the magic moments'. Have a look at them. They're bizarre – but then so is the company's geyser-like rise in earnings.

29. Pack up, collect rubbish
30. 8 minute special task – this can be anything from fixing a child's toy to mending a screen door.
31. Replace light bulbs if required – this is usually done for free
32. Power socket protectors if required
33. Set timers on electronic devices
34. Check roof for problems
35. Sweep cobwebs
36. Straighten doormat when leaving
37. Straighten and hang pictures
38. Mend or oil hinges
39. Remove weeds on pavement
40. Leave cheerfully

No wonder he doesn't need to advertise!

I showed the list to some domestic cleaners who whined, 'But we don't get paid what those guys earn on a security system'.

'No', I agreed but they don't come back every week like you do either. They only come once in a lifetime. You could develop a WE CARE list of one hundred actions and do them over a two year period. Just mark your invoice, *Rake leaves – no charge.*

In a retail store it could be as simple as:
'Sauce is free today.'
'Ties are half price with shirts this afternoon.'
'Have a free newspaper with your book. Pretend it's your birthday.'
'If you buy two cookies with your coffee I'll pop a muffin in a bag for your supper.'
'Suits dry cleaned free every three months.'
'Tyres rotated and balanced free every 5,000 Kilometres.'

3. Service it before it breaks

The Daichi company sends owners a letter to say most electronic equipment breaks down after the warranty period is over. The letter explains that the customer's product will be out of warranty soon and as repairs could be costly it might be a good idea to have the product checked for free while it is still under warranty just in case any fault is looming. Any repairs could be performed free of charge as per the agreement.

How do you think it would affect you if you got a letter like that in the mail?

I know. You'd be suspicious that they were up to something wouldn't you. *They are up to something*. It's called Five Star Service and building trust.

4. First cut free

Bill Vis, founder of VIP Home Services built his empire on 'Your first lawn cut free'.

I remember when 16 trailers pulled up outside my house opposite his for Friday afternoon check-in. Now there are over one thousand franchisees in two countries.

5. Love letter

Bob Jane offers $195 worth of service and discount vouchers free, when you get two new tyres and a wheel alignment.
The little yellow tyre and safety plan booklet is the backbone of bonding you to your local Bob Jane T-Mart store. I call it their love letter.

Why? It keeps you coming back to get the great free service and top deals. While you are there they can offer you their other premium balancing services and wheels.

Activity: Draw up a list of leave-'em-begging-for-more things you could do for your customers, apart from the list you made in the last lesson to go with your service promise.

FIVE STAR IDEA:
Become a legend in someone else's lunch time and see how much you can do to keep and grow your customers' business.

LESSON 32

Love your products

Sell your own brands

You get your customers to come back to you for top quality advice and long-term service when you lock them into your own brands.

How's this for dumb?

I'd been given some specialty vitamins by a friend who thought I needed them and when I'd finished the bottle I asked The Lovely Christine to pick up some more when she was ducking off to the shops one day. (She's always 'ducking' off to the shops.) Being specialty vitamins they came from a specialty store.

She called into the store and asked one of the employees for a replacement bottle of their own brand.

The salesperson (I use the term loosely) said, 'They're not very good. You should get these', and convinced her to buy another brand altogether which happened to be cheaper.

You can buy these cheaper at the supermarket.

Are we happy customers?

I suppose we were happy. To me at that time vitamins were vitamins, and I didn't really give a fig about one milligram more or less of this or that.

I am more worried now about the store owners.

You see the brand the woman sold us can be purchased anywhere. Next time we're at the big supermarket or the pharmacy we will see the brand she sold us and pop a bottle in the trolley with all our other shopping items.

Besides that, their 'own brand' must have higher margins so there's more profit to be made, but of course our altruistic employee thinks profit is evil – until we suggest the loss in profit be deducted from her pay packet. Then she becomes very capitalistic indeed!

Send me away. It costs you nothing except your job

So instead of selling me an item with the specialty shop's brand emblazoned on it, screaming at me to go back there every time I open the bottle, she sold me an advertisement for someone else's business. Her boss and the other participants in the chain had spent a fortune in advertising to get us to shop there in the first place but in one stupid move had suggested we need never return.

When the bottle is empty it goes in the 'get some more' box in the kitchen. The only place we should be able to get some more is back at the specialty store.

The customer misses out on everything – not just the pills

But we can now get a 'better' brand at the supermarket. We will never need to go back to the specialty store so will not become a lifetime customer for those vitamins but worse than that we will never again present them with an opportunity to sell us their muesli ingredients, their magic milk substitutes, their enchanted footwear, their foot powders, low allergen shampoos and conditioners, herbal teas, soothing balms, healing emollients, and calming oils. And we won't be bringing our friends back to get that fabulous five star service either.

Who's at fault?

Everyone is to blame.

The employee hasn't shown the slightest courtesy for the employer's business and doesn't realise that their own job security is directly related to repeat sales.

The employers haven't paid attention to the day-to-day business skills of the team. They've just employed shop assistants to be in the shop; highly qualified, gifted, attractive, conscientious lard heads.

FIVE STAR IDEA:
Show every employee the cash drawer and explain that their wages can only come out of it if they put customers' money in it – visit after visit after visit. Explain that the best customer service is the kind that brings the customer back to YOU, because you give the best service. (You do don't you?)

LESSON 33

No dissin' your own brands!

Definition: dissin' = abbreviated form of *dissing*, a colloquialised form of *disrespecting*. eg. *Don't diss my car man!*

They dissed your brands Man!

A manager told me about the time a customer rang to report two of his silly store managers.

> The client had just purchased a huge supply of some special manchester items which were labelled in his store's brand name. The products were identical to the manufacturer's premium brand, simply re-packaged.
>
> The customer had bought some of these items and for whatever reason was not happy with her purchase – the hems were crooked or something minor.
>
> She took the items back to another store in the chain and pointed out the bad workmanship.
>
> The manager told her she needed to get them replaced at the store where they'd been purchased, but pointed out that there had been a lot of problems with the items. 'She "dissed" your brands Man.'
>
> The salesperson said, 'They're not that good actually. We had them made ourselves.'

The customer trotted off to the original store and highlighted the mistakes once more. This store manager also offered some lifesaving 'dissing'.

'Yes, none of us are happy with them. Would you do us all a favour and complain to head office?'

The customer did complain – and did some 'dissing' about the disloyal twits the manager employs.

'How can they rubbish their own product?' asked the customer. 'It's like throwing your children on the street. It was only a little thing but they panicked and turned it into a major dispute with their management.'

FIVE STAR IDEA:
Teach the staff to value the business they work in and protect it like they protect their own family. Take products back and offer a reward for the complaint but don't join in the complaint. It doesn't make them look like heroes. It makes them look stupid.

LESSON 34

FREQUENT FLYER MILES, INCH BY INCH

I had a teacher at school who only had one joke.

He'd say, 'It's the little things that make a difference. Pearce! Take your brain for instance.' It was terribly hilarious.

He was right about one thing. Little things count. Tom Peters and Nancy Waterman told us that successful customer relations are built up inch by inch; a thousand thousand things done right. Tragically, years of painstaking work can be set back miles by one small indiscretion.

> I have a preferred airline and covet my gold frequent flyer status, which includes access to the airport lounge.
>
> A client booked me on the rival airline recently to connect with an international flight. I approached the domestic lounge staff and asked if my international business ticket entitled me to access the international lounge as it did on 'my' airline. It seemed like a simple question but none of five staff could come up with an answer.
>
> Once on the plane I watched a steward ask a first-class customer to hand over her (oversized) handbag. The passenger did not understand the danger of carrying a large bag on her lap so the steward raised her voice and said 'It's for safety madam!'

The passenger handed over her bag and as the steward placed it in the overhead locker behind the view of the passenger, opened her mouth wide and made a cat-like hiss at the passenger.

These two puny incidents were enough to reassure me that my choice of airline was justified.

. I'm sure you could tell me plenty of similar stories about my preferred airline or all airlines in general, so I'm not suggesting that mine is better than yours.

I am simply pointing out that any hope of getting me to spend my $100,000 per year with the other airline is an unrealistic ambition.

My airline has built a relationship with me over many years and many flights. Inch by inch they have earned my loyalty. These days I overlook their faults and know what to expect.

Having seen how far the other airline has to go I can't face the agony of getting used to them inch by inch.

It ought to be that way for your customers. They should be so used to being loved by you; the way you remind them of special events; the way you offer them preferential service for loyalty; the way you recover from mistakes; that they could not bear to go through the agony of changing to another store or supplier.

It's like they should be able to waltz into your store any time of day or night and order 'the usual', whatever that is for you, and know they can get it.

Homoeopathic doses

You build that trust in them inch by inch – centimetre by centimetre – gram by gram with daily homoeopathic doses of kindness, attention, love, faithfulness and patience. You always have their product in the store or you get it for them fast. You call them in advance to say you will be late with a delivery.

A pharmacist won our family's business by offering to courier our filled prescriptions to our house. He calls and asks if we would like anything else included; toothpaste, shampoo, throat lozenges, lip balm – anything. The parcel always arrives with free samples of new products he's recommending.

The pharmacist wanted your opinion on a few samples.

FIVE STAR IDEA:
Get out your key customer list and run a check over the little things you could do to make sure they stay loyal to you. Could you write to them, ring them up, send them a post card, send them a gift, offer them a preferential price or treatment – just because you like them – not because you want to sell them something?

LESSON 35

Pareto, Prato, Brian from the Footy Club and the 80:20 rule

Who said that?

The father of fascism, the French industrialist and intellectual, Vilfredo Pareto (1848-1923), is credited with the Pareto Principle. So is the non-existent Greek philosopher Prato and so is a chap down at the footy club called Brian. In fact you could become famous for it yourself if you liked.

It doesn't matter who named the phenomenon. It's there. And it's like the weather: Everyone complains about it but nobody does anything about it.

> 'The old 80:20 rule', says Brian down at the footy club, 'means that for any working bee, 20% of the members do 80% of the work. Only 20% of the members make extra contributions to the fund-raiser nights. Only 20% of the members roll up to the Annual General Meeting. The rest are drunks.'

Only 20% of the customers take part in the lamington drives.

If you analyse your business you'll find a figure like this lurking around in the back of your computer or receipt book. There's a number of people who are keeping you going but it's unlikely to be everyone who comes in. Depending on the nature of your business, you will probably discover that you have some core customers who keep you fed. It might not be as low as 20%. It might be lower.

Waste of energy

Like Brian at the footy club, you might also discover that the others waste 80% of your time and energy. 'We spend all our time ringing them up and sending them reminders to come to things only to see the same old faces time after time. It makes me wonder why we do it.' We could run the footy club just as well without them.

Waste of space

And then you might find that you have some core products too. 80% of your sales might be in only 20% of product categories and lines. Brian at the footy club says, 'The canteen does a roaring trade in pies and Cokes. Your fancy cakes and your lemonades are for your little old lady or little kid. Same with bags of mixed sweets. Waste of space. You end up giving them to the kindergarten.'

Analyse sales

If you analyse sales you might discover that the 20% of the people who give you 80% of your revenue only spend in 20% of your range.

This could be revealing and challenging. What's the good of bragging in your brochure that you have 2,500 lines when 80% of your revenue comes from only 500 lines. On further examination you discover that your 'throw out' table is always used to dump items from the remaining 2,000 lines.

Are you saying, 'But we're a variety store. We need variety.'

*No you don't need variety. You need **viability***. You won't be viable unless you sell what the buyers with the most money and the highest frequency want to buy.

It makes me mad. They only buy business suits.

Get radical

I hear someone saying, 'But the 80% stock lines are where my profit comes from. I couldn't survive on only 20% of them. People would think my shop was empty.'

Balderdash! I'm saying that when you find out what your best customers buy, you'll get to choose from four options and you'll find out that your costs, not your profits, come from 80% of your product lines.

Options - choose one or all

1. Stock more of those 20% hot lines to entice the spenders in.
2. Look for more customers like your best 20% to take up the slack.
3. Cut out the wasteful product lines.
4. Cut the wasteful overheads in wasteful advertising to sell the

wasteful product lines AND the wasteful staffing to manage the wasteful product lines AND the wasteful space to stock the wasteful product lines AND ... enjoy the profits.

Maybe I'm wrong in your case

It could turn out that you have 2,000 customers who spend $2 each a week and they spend it on 2,000 different items. Call me on reverse charges and tell me about it. Also tell me where you buried the pot of gold you found at the end of the rainbow and how Santa Claus and the Easter Bunny were the last time you had tea and funny mushroom cakes with them.

Analyse customers

What about keeping close records of the buying patterns of your key customers. Look into their frequency of purchase and their average sale. Track the style of product they buy.

This is where you can begin to make some strategic buying decisions. Instead of buying every fandangle the trade reps tell you to buy, only buy what you know you can sell at the highest profit to the people who are your main source of revenue.

Patience is needed. This might take you a few years to find out. But please stop jamming your store with doo dads and gee gaws just hoping that suckers will stroll in and want it and somehow you'll get rich – unless of course this is working for you so far.

Hey! Ask them what they want to buy from your store. Hand out or mail out fact finders. Here's a starter sample for a menswear store questionnaire:

Hello.

We like having you as a customer and want to keep having you come back to our store. Could you tell us what you'd like to buy from us?

Tick a box

☐ Pairs of socks in the price range $4-$7

☐ Thicker

☐ Thinner

☐ Longer

☐ Shorter

☐ Packs of socks in the price range $10-$15, $15-$20

☐ Thicker

☐ Thinner

☐ Longer

☐ Shorter

☐ Business shirts

☐ White

☐ Blue

☐ Patterns/stripes

☐ Jeans

☐ Colours – light dark stone washed

☐ Styles – pleated, hipsters, front pocket, side pocket

Why?

'Why?' you may well ask. Why do I want you to separate the 80 from the 20? Well quite simply put, this is the only way you can render five star service. You do the best you can for the people who will appreciate it most. You don't thrash your brains out trying to be all things to all people. You simply cannot offer five star service to every Dick, Tom and Harriet who pops by for a cursory sticky beak in your window.

I'm not advocating disrespect or disdain. You know that by now. You can offer four star service, or three star service or even two star service – always polite, kind and servant hearted but you must serve best where your efforts will be rewarded most. It's a business, not a charity. This is one of the hardest lines for me to draw for you. Every fibre of my being tells me to tell you to serve all people equally, but that will not work in your chosen field. You must be discerning.

FIVE STAR IDEA:
Maximise your strengths. Minimise your weaknesses.

LESSON 36

Understand the ladder

David Ogilvy, the prince of the advertising kingdom is reputed to have thought up the ladder of customer loyalty so I'll give him the glory. I've been putting my own spin on it for about twelve years now so that I have actually forgotten how it started so apologies to Mr. Ogilvy's fans.

You need to understand the ladder to really appreciate the nature of retailer-customer relationships.

Theory says that there are five levels of loyalty in a customer's relationship with you:

Advocate
Client
Customer
Shopper
Prospect
Suspect

A Suspect has no loyalty

These people are not even on the ladder and have never experienced your service so they know nothing about you and could just as easily walk into any opposition store to spend their hard-won government hand out. They even walk into your store and look around. They finger the merchandise, but they are not prospects. They are just killing time waiting for the bus.

A prospect has marginal loyalty

Suspects are turned into prospects by several occurrences.

They develop a genuine need for your product or service.
They see your advertising and their desire to own your product is awakened.
They hear about you from another happy customer.
They inherit you from a parent or employer.
They are referred to you by a specialist in a related field.

You shouldn't let these people off the phone without making an appointment or out of the store without parting with their cash.

A spender is only a casual acquaintance

I threw this one into Mr. Ogilvy's list.
Most of your 'customers' are not customers at all. They are merely people buying things. The word 'spender' defines the passing trade, the drop-in browser, the impulse buyer. They buy from you today and from the shop down the road tomorrow and could take you or leave you. They have not earned the right to be called customers yet and that is largely your responsibility. You have not won a high enough level of loyalty from them.

Activity: List a few categories of people you notice who could be best described as spenders – casual buyers.

A customer is a creature of habit

By definition a customer buys from you *as a custom.* They make a habit of spending with you. They expect you to carry their favourite items. They arrive at the same time of day or at the same time of week. They form habit patterns which they don't like to break. This person is more loyal but they are not yet married to you. It will not take much to bring the last level of loyalty out of them.

Activity: List a few people who fit the category of 'customer'. You might not know some of them by name (yet) but you can at least list them by groupings – age, hours at which they come eg. lunch, morning tea.

A client depends on you alone

From the French word *lien* 'to rely on' or 'lean on' we get our understanding of what it means to have clients. Clients are very special and most businesses would be lucky to have more than a handful in a lifetime. Accountants and lawyers being the swanks they are have carefully picked the nicest word out of the language of commerce and decided to call their spenders and customers *clients* when they may not be clients at all. Departments of correctional services glamorise the offenders in their care by calling them 'clients' too. I'm not comforted by this.

Clients need you, your products and your services. They cannot run their businesses or their lives without you and without you alone. If that's the relationship you enjoy with your clients then go ahead and call them clients. If not, then they are merely spenders or customers and it is your job to woo them up the ladder.

Why? There is a sea of ladders and they are easy to fall off. You also earn more money from clients and advocates. This is the 20% group from Lesson 32.

Activity: List your clients. Be honest now. List your real clients.

____

____

____

____

____

Advocates send you more business – but they're queue jumpers

Advocates are the hardest to pin down. Theoretically in the neat box of definitions, a person moves through the first five levels and after dealing with you for a time becomes your best advertisement and tells the world about the wonderful lifelong relationship they've had with you. They advocate you to others after having been a spender, then a customer and then a client.

But advocacy is a strange condition that makes people jump the queue.

- People who have never been in your store can be advocates. They know of your reputation and recommend that friends or family spend with you.
- People who have heard about you on the radio can send people to you. You sound convincing or you sound as though you have a solution.
- People who have only been in your store for a stickybeak can send people to you. They liked what they saw and excitedly tell others as if they are 'in the know.'
- People who have only spent with you once could tell dozens of people about you. It might have been such a great experience that they can't help ring the radio talk back show brag about you or to tell the gang down at the bowls club. This is more likely to be so if you sell once in a lifetime products or larger ticket items.

Reward you advocates

The best advocates however are those you know about. You reward them with gifts, cards, special premium offers, invitations to product releases and the football grand final. You love them more and they love you more and 'here we go 'round the mulberry bush'.

But all I did was send Grandma in for a blue rinse.

When was the last time your lawyer or accountant took you to the footy or a ball because you were his 'client'? If he has never done it then you can be sure he doesn't really think you are a client even though he includes you in his client head count when he assesses the value of his business. He doesn't take his little spenders does he? He only takes his big spenders. They might not be clients either!

You have to be careful to unpack the word and treat the relationship accordingly.

Activity: What are you doing to move people up the ladder?
1. Segment your 'visitors' into the rungs on the ladder.

How many people do you have in each category?

What is each section worth to you? (It could be that your spenders are worth more than your customers, but I doubt it.)

CATEGORY		VALUE
Advocates	____________	________
	____________	________
	____________	________
Client	____________	________
	____________	________
	____________	________
Customer	____________	________
	____________	________
	____________	________
Spenders	____________	________
	____________	________
	____________	________

Prospect Interesting question. Worth nothing at the moment but what COULD they be worth?

____________ ________

Is it possible to move people up the ladder? (In your business it may not be.)

2. If you believe it is possible and worthwhile to target some specific individuals or groups and strategise how to move them to the next level.

Names	Plans
________	____________________
________	____________________
________	____________________
________	____________________

LESSON 37

UNDERSTAND THE RIDDLE OF POWER, SKILL AND FLEXIBILITY

How many times in this book have I said that something is the key to Five Star Service? This is another one of those concepts.

It's a strange riddle:

The more skill and power you have, the less flexible you can be.
The more flexibility you're required to exercise, the more power you seem to assume but with less skill.
The more skilfully you use your flexibility the less power you need but the more you have.

Consider a few examples.

All Skill and power. No flexibility.

Brain surgeon: A brain surgeon operating on you has absolute power over life and death and of all the surgeons perhaps possesses the ultimate skill. At the same time she can exercise no flexibility at all. She can't decide to add bits of monkey brain to fill in holes and can't take out a few bulgy bits to even things up. She is guided by absolute rigid rules of anatomy, surgery and ethics. Her five star service is exhibited in her unyielding inflexibility.

Rocket scientist: The precision of maths and physics skills needed to land people on the moon or to put them in orbit around Mars is almost impossible to comprehend. One millimetre of misjudgment between here and the clouds doesn't seem much, but it could mean the difference between getting some nice snapshots of Mars and helplessly orbiting Alpha Centauri for the next Bilennium. The rocket scientist is not at liberty to fly over his house to wave at the kids on his way back either. It's total power, maximum skill and NO flexibility for Andy Astronaut.

Let me break this to you as gently as I can. Customer service is not rocket science and you ain't no brain surgeon. In comparison with the two professions I've mentioned you and I have limited skill and hardly any power but we are loaded with opportunities for flexibility. It's the way we exercise that flexibility that marks out the measure of our Five Star Service. It's the Ric Angeletti factor.

You should have turned right at Albuquerqe.

Flexibility with minimal skill and assumed power

The school crossing monitor: The nasty old bloke at the school crossing stands there holding back the tiny tots facing a road devoid of traffic except for your car. You are late for a meeting but you slow down to respect the school speed zone. You cannot believe it as the guard puts whistle to lips and blows you to a halt when it would be as easier to let you pass. The job takes no skill at all when compared with the brain surgeon's level of training. There's not much difference between blowing a whistle and the death test: ie. seeing if he's alive by holding a mirror under his nose to see if his breathing fogs it.

He had all the flexibility in the world to let you drive on through, but chose to exercise power unnecessarily.

The postage stamp seller: You need to send your Grandmother in England a gift for Christmas and it is one minute before closing time on the last day for shipping. The postage is seven dollars and forty three cents rounded up to forty five but you only have seven dollars and forty cents.
'You need the extra five cents', she says.
You say, 'So how about rounding it down to forty instead of rounding it up to forty five',
'Nope. Already entered it in the computer. It'll be out by three cents.'
'Do you have five cents you can lend me?'
'If I lent everyone five cents I'd be broke. You should carry extra change. Anyway if you haven't got it, you can't post it and we're closed now. Come back tomorrow.'

These relatively skill-less tasks take on life from the Dark Side when they are handled with absolute power and no flexibility. This is where the lousiest examples of bad customer service come from.

All power to the person with no power, minimal skill but maximum flexibility

The tram driver: This man is the 'act' on Melbourne's tourist ride around the city. He was wisely chosen for his jovial personality. I saw him one summer's day on a tram, sardine-packed with both tourists and locals. All the way around the circle route he kept me spell-bound with his side show. He ran the tram like a tourist bus, chattering from his cabin about the city sights to whoever could hear him. No matter who hopped on the tram he seemed to be able to guess their country of birth and jabber a few words of greeting in their native tongue. He stopped the tram to let people on where there were no stops, and let them off wherever was closest to where they wanted to go. 'Thy should have more stops near things you want to see', he'd say. It was nothing to stop the tram to let parents with prams cross in front of him.

He'd wave at the toddlers and ding his bell. Yet the traffic wasn't snarled up behind the tram and the passengers all arrived at their destinations at about the same time as if he'd rushed.

The most memorable incident was when our party of nine had got off and were walking along the footpath. The tram stopped one hundred metres in front of us and he came running back along the road waving something and shouting, 'You forgot your sunnies'.

'Not ours', we called out.

He kept running. 'Are you sure? Check everyone.'
We checked but the sun glasses were not ours. He turned around and ran back to his tram.
'Never mind', he laughed, 'I'll keep driving around the city ringing my bell till the owner works it out.'
Where does a tram driver get the flair to perform like that? Easy. He's answered the riddle. They who have no power and minimal skill perform the best acts of Five Star Service when they are the most flexible.

The thing that drives most of us quite mad is service providers who are rule bound, fog bound and mud hole bound.

Activity:
1. Analyse your service patterns and see if there are places where you could be more flexible but you like to play demigod instead.

2. Are there areas where it is dangerous for you to exercise flexibility? eg maverick discounts or 'gifts' that cost the business profit? Lay out some boundaries so that everyone knows what your business believes about flexibility. Then be flexible about it.

LESSON 38

WHAT'S IT TAKE TO ACHIEVE GREATNESS?

Act now!

I have made hundreds of suggestions and given dozens of examples in this book. You will find none that requires either genius or gold to implement. There is however not one suggestion that you could not implement within a week.

You might have found all the suggestions overwhelming and don't know how you will put them all into practice so here's what I recommend. Start with the first activity at the end of lesson one, and when you have completed that, go on one by one to all the others.

Here it is again:

FIVE STAR IDEA:
Whether you're the CEO or the cleaner – even the door person – open your mind and ask if there is the slightest possibility that you could find a way you can turn your job into an all-singing, all-dancing, star-studded, thrill-a-minute performance?

You have the time.

A legacy

In lesson 25, I asked you to think about what legacy you will leave your community and your industry when you finally move on. I conclude this book with testimony to one such legacy.

> I had lunch yesterday with David Cook, a Bob Jane T-Mart franchisee, whose young manager, Callin Gill died in a road accident about ten months ago. I told Dave I'd heard that it had been a hard time for him and that I admired how he'd carried himself through it all.
>
> He choked several times as he spoke about how Callin had died delivering a customer's car after hours on a Friday night. It was typical of the favours Callin did for his customers. As team leader, Callin had been the core of Dave's business culture and one by one the other team members had quietly left the business because they said it just wasn't the same any more without Callin. Customers had fallen away too because he had been so wonderful to them. Dave regarded losing Callin, (the 'lovable rogue', he called him) as one of the great tragedies of his life. Callin had a truly intuitive feel for what was best for the business, the team and the customers.
>
> To his immense credit and enduring spirit, after a long struggle Dave had built a new team and a new culture and had won some old customers back and wooed many new ones. He has faced many dark hours and days yet he had nowhere else to go but onward and upward, so he did.
>
> I grew up in a tyre fitting family. It's not a glamorous job. Yet like my Dad Callin showed that any job, if carried out with heart and

dedication, can be as significant an occupation as the so-called noblest of callings.

The touching conversation with Dave reminded me that Callin had been a true Five Star performer and his epitaph is written on the hearts of all who worked with him and were served by him.

FIVE STAR IDEA:
Let the one who would be greatest among you, first be humble and become the servant of many.

How to get more successful selling ideas

It's easy!

1. More copies of the book are available now so that you can use them as training tools for your team.

2. The double audio cassette pack ***"Five Star Service on a One Star Budget"*** covers all the material in this book with live interviews and comments. It will add profit generating insights into the ideas you have picked up in this book.

3. Choose the other packages of audio tapes to complete your selling skills library.

4. Colin speaks at conventions and seminars all over the world. He might be available in your neighbourhood just when you need him. His laugh-a-minute presentations reinforce everything you've read in this book and your people will find his style refreshing and stimulating — but more to the point, you will find your sales and service levels step up to the next level.

5. The first book in this series is still available. You should get that book as well to make your Retail Success Series complete.

6. Visit our web site for extensive information about selling. It is called The World Sales Center because that best describes its purpose – to be the absolute centre of information about anything to do with selling:

http://www.worldsalescenter.com

How to get your copies

Retailers in Westfield centres can order the book easily:

If you are a retailer in a Westfield shopping centre simply pick up the phone and call the centre management and put in your order for however many books you wish to purchase. They will be happy to talk to you about special prices for bulk orders.

If you're NOT in a Westfield centre, or you want the tapes, contact World Sales Center direct and use the order form at the back:

CALL: +618 8374-0711
FAX: +618 8374-2433
E-MAIL: cjp@worldsalescenter.com
Check out our web site: http://www.worldsalescenter.com
POST: Box 303 UNLEY South Australia 5061

Five Star Service on a One Star Budget – Double Cassette set $30
The tape set gives you the perfect companion to this book. Hear Colin teach the key ideas in the book and listen to live interviews with the Five Star performers you've been reading about. Once you've read the book you can get the reinforcement you need using these audio cassettes as a different teaching medium. this way the message is always fresh. You can also share the tapes with your team to reinforce the ideas you want them to use.

Make More Money From Every Sale – Book $20
You CAN make more in your business without spending a cent on advertising, or attracting new customers. Read your own copy of the first book in the Retail Success Series to learn how to sell more to the customers you already have. It's easy. You'll find out

- You CAN make more money from every sale
- Why you DON'T make more money from every sale
- Why you SHOULD make more money from every sale
- HOW you CAN make more money from every sale.

Make More Money From Every Sale – Cassette. $30 Includes free bonus tape 'Selling Isn't Telling' which itself is valued at $29. Ever wondered how add-on selling really works? Use the proven, profit-making ideas on these tapes to increase your business . . . overnight! When you know how, making money from add-on selling isn't a mystery. It is simple, smart business practice. This tape gives you the win/win you've been looking for . . . *happy customers and bigger sales!*

Get to No 1 in Sales & Stay There – 6 cassette pack. $125
Seize the Winning Edge! When you can sell, you have More money – More power – More control over your life!

- Say less! And make every word a winner.
- Identify your prospect so you don't waste time.
- Handle objections with S.A.SH.M.A.C.
- Close so your customers say 'YES'!
- Use P.E.A.R.C.E.S. benefit formula to make your product absolutely irresistible.
- Read your customers and make a winning first impression.

Manage & Lead Without Losing Sleep – Cassette $30 Includes free bonus tape 'Off the Wardrobe' which itself is valued at $29. Want to feel in control – of today and the future? You will, when you understand how to be a great leader and an outstanding manager. Now you'll achieve your objectives without pressure, without stress and with more control! This practical no-nonsense tape gives you a whole new understanding of the 13 characteristics of leadership and management you need to run your organisation successfully.

Keep Your Customers Happy on the Phone Super profit-making double cassette set! $60

Embarrassed by the image of your business? Now, you'll have the perfect answer. Use these tapes to win more business and make more sales. You'll be amazed at the difference when you and your staff know what to say and how to say it.

- 7 reasons why your organisation must become flawless on the phone.
- 6 rules you can't neglect if you don't want to lose another customer.

Make People Really Listen to You $30

Includes free bonus tape 'G.I. Deon' – which itself is valued at $29.

Really want people to get your message? They will, when you use the powerful speaking and communication skills on these tapes. Learn how to hold your audience. More importantly, learn how to communicate so that your message is well remembered. Now, as a speaker, you'll really make a difference!

Bright Ideas Newsletter $72 Monthly newsletter tightly packed with useable information and ideas, so you can absorb them and pass them on quickly – 12 month subscription.

To World Sales Center:

Box 303 UNLEY South Australia 5061
Fax: +618 8374-2433

Yes! Please send me

Copies	Title	Code	Unit cost	Amount
	Five Star Service on a One Star Budget (book)	BK02	$20	
	Five Star Service on a One Star Budget (double cassette pack)	BT11	$30	
	Make More Money from Every Sale (book)	BK01	$20	
	Make More Money from Every Sale (double cassette pack)	BT10	$30	
	Get to No 1 in Sales & Stay There (six cassette pack)	BT01	$125	
	Manage & Lead Without Losing Sleep (double cassette pack)	BT08	$30	
	Keep Your Customers Happy on the Phone (double cassette pack)	BT03	$60	
	Make People Really Listen (double cassette pack)	BT02	$30	
	Bright Ideas (12 month subscription)	BN01	$72 per year	
Postal orders in Australia include $4:00 P&H. Orders outside Australia subject to air freight. Call for special prices and freight rates on bulk orders.				
			Total A$	

My name is ______________________ Position ______________________

Organisation ______________________

Address ______________________ Code __________

Phone __________ Fax __________ e-mail __________

☐ Cheque enclosed ***OR*** ☐ Credit card

☐ AMEX (ID No.   ) ☐ VISA ☐ MASTERCARD

☐☐☐☐ ☐☐☐☐ ☐☐☐☐ ☐☐☐☐

Exp date __________ Signature ______________________